Emergent Computer Literacy

Routledge Research in Education

Emergent Computer Literacy

A Developmental Perspective

Helen Mele Robinson

Routledge
Taylor & Francis Group
New York   London

First published 2009
by Routledge
270 Madison Ave, New York, NY 10016

Simultaneously published in the UK
by Routledge
2 Park Square, Milton Park, Abingdon, Oxon OX14 4RN

Routledge is an imprint of the Taylor & Francis Group, an informa business

© 2009 Taylor & Francis

Typeset in Sabon by IBT Global.
Printed and bound in the United States of America on acid-free paper by IBT Global.

Library of Congress Cataloging in Publication Data
Robinson, Helen Mele.
   Emergent computer literacy : a developmental perspective / by Helen Mele Robinson.
      p. cm. — (Routledge research in education ; 20)
   Includes bibliographical references and index.
   1. Computer literacy.   I. Title.
   QA76.9.C64R63 2009
   004—dc22
                                       2008020541

ISBN10: 0-415-96131-9 (hbk)
ISBN10: 0-203-88791-3 (ebk)

ISBN13: 978-0-415-96131-8 (hbk)
ISBN13: 978-0-203-88791-2 (ebk)

This book is dedicated to my children Nicole, Leland, and Rachel. As I have watched them grow and interact with computers they have taught me so much. Through their eyes I have learned about the world of technology.

Contents

Figures

Tables

Prologue

Computers entered my world when I was already an adult and I am mainly self-taught. I am what Marc Prensky (2001a) refers to as a digital immigrant. I am comfortable with computers and technology, willing to experiment, and have made accommodations to successfully exist in a digital world. However I have not assimilated fully with computers and technology which I demonstrate with my use of archaic strategies such as printing out emails. My own duality of existing in a world before computers and now in a world surrounded by computers, adds to my understanding of the subject.

My experience with children and computers began in the 1980s. As an Early Childhood Director, with the help of parent fundraising, I was able to introduce computers into the nursery classes of my school in a developmentally appropriate manner. During this time as a parent I offered my own three children access to a computer in the home setting. Therefore, over the years, I have experienced children interacting with computers in the home setting and in the school setting.

My doctoral work at Fordham University brought together my interest of language, literacy, and learning with computers. I became intrigued with how young children grasp the skills to eventually interact independently with computers. In a pilot study for my dissertation, I observed five-year-old children attempting to use computers in the home setting with parental guidance. For my dissertation, I went on to study six-year-old children who could function more independently with scaffolding from their parents. The findings of this study offer implications for adults guiding children with computers in both home and educational settings. While conducting this research, I also began to recognize the analogy between emergent literacy and the acquisition of computer knowledge.

This book is the culmination of observations and research gathered over the last two decades. Many questions have been answered; however, many still remain. How does a person build his or her computer knowledge and learn to use computer hardware or software? What is the impact on the learning process when more experienced peers or adults interact with children? This book is an initial response to the many questions that are raised when trying to understand how children acquire computer knowledge, both independently and with adult guidance.

Acknowledgments

My thanks to the study families who welcomed me into their homes to observe, record, and learn about children using computers for my research project. Without their cooperation this study would not have been possible.

I would like to express my gratitude to my family and friends for their encouragement and support during the process of developing my dissertation into a research-based book. My sincere thanks to Rachel Robinson for the feedback she offered during revisions for the ever-changing topic of young children and computers. Finally, a special thanks to my husband, Nick Robinson, who believed in me as a writer and gave me the impetus to complete my project.

1 Introduction

Computers, video games, cell phones, and Blu-ray Disc players are the toys and tools that many American children of all ages use on a daily basis. American society has moved from the Industrial Age of the 19th century to the Information Age of today. During the transition to the Information Age "an economy built on knowledge rather than goods and services began to emerge" (Bitter & Pierson, 2002, p. 2). The 21st century will turn out to be the period of America's greatest preeminence and the United States is better positioned than any other country to multiply the potency of its power resources through information (Nye & Owens, 1996). How prepared American children are for the challenge of entering the technological workforce will impact the status of the United States as a world power.

Technology as referring "primarily to computer technology" (National Association for the Education of Young Children [NAEYC], 1996, p. 1) is pervasive in American society. In examining the topic of young children and computers, the discussion needs to emanate from a definition of what a computer is. "Technically, a computer is a programmable machine. This means it can execute a programmed list of instructions and respond to new instructions that it is given. Today, however, the term is most often used to refer to the desktop and laptop computers that most people use" (Tech-Terms.com, 2008, ¶ 1). To begin to think about the topic of young children and computers, the issue of children acquiring language and literacy skills needs to be understood. The adults in a child's environment offer guidance to enable acquisition of language and literacy skills, and when ready, computer literacy. Wasik, Dobbins, and Herrmann (2002, p. 444) offer the conventional definition of literacy as, "one's ability to read and write." In the 21st century there is an expansion on the definition of literacy as, "the abilities of individuals to read, write, speak, listen, view, and think" (Cooper, 2000, p. 6). This perspective of literacy influences how parents guide their children to be prepared to become productive young adults able to succeed in the workforce. Parents assist a child's language expansion by talking to, talking with, and role modeling language skills for their children (Shonkoff & Phillips, 2000). In the home setting, parents or those who serve the parenting role in a child's life provide role modeling and guide children in the development of reading and writing skills. In school settings teachers provide direct instruction, role modeling, and overall guidance for continued growth of language and literacy skills.

What computer knowledge are children expected to attain to be ready for their role as citizens in American society? What does it mean to be computer literate? The meaning of the phrase has changed many times since originally being coined in 1972 by Arthur Luehrmann in his discussion of computers as a rising essential element in educational environments (Moursund, 2003). The definition of computer literacy has been debated since the 1970s (Deringer & Molnar, 1982) when the National Science Foundation was asked by the President of the United States, Richard M. Nixon, and Congress to offer leadership for computers in education in our country. In 1980 the view of researchers was that "a computer literate populace is as necessary to an information society as raw materials and energy are to an industrial society" (p. 3). In the 1980s, a definition of computer literacy had been proposed by researchers ranging from Moursund (1982) with a view of computer literacy as "a working knowledge of computers" (p. 83), to a broader common definition of computer literacy purported by Watt (1982) as primarily a body of information about computers, how computers work, how computers are used, and the impact of computers on society.

Moursund's (2003) current definition of computer literacy is "a functional level of knowledge and skills in using computers and computer-based multimedia as an aid to communication with oneself and others for the purposes of learning, knowing, and for using one's knowledge" (p. 9). Roblyer (2003) has recently offered the view of computer literacy as the skill required for using information technology in education and in the workplace. The definition of computer literacy proposed by Computer Literacy USA (CL-USA) (2007) is that computer literacy is:

> An understanding of the concepts, terminology and operations that relate to general computer use. It is the essential knowledge needed to function independently with a computer. This functionality includes the ability to solve and avoid problems, adapt to new situations, keep information organized and communicate effectively with other computer literate people. (p. 1)

The description offered by CL-USA is the definition that will be employed for the current study. An understanding and definition of the term computer literacy offers a perspective that frames the strategies for adults guiding children's growing awareness of how to use a computer.

In American society computers are becoming ubiquitous as part of daily life (Shields & Behrman, 2000). Computer technology and thriving in an environment where computers are used seem to be necessary understandings for children to develop. To prepare young children for future educational endeavors, as well as integration into a technological society, guidance and acquisition of computer knowledge needs to be part of a child's learning experience (Roblyer, 2003).

In the 1970s early childhood educators and parents debated whether computers were here to stay (Armstrong & Casement, 2000). In the 1980s parents and teachers realized that computers were the wave of the future and the debate turned to whether it was appropriate to use computers with young children (Haugland & Wright, 1997). By the end of the 1990s computer technology had clearly become an integral part of American society in daily life, the business world, and education. There seems to be clear and widespread agreement among the public and educators that students need to be proficient computer users: Students need to be computer literate (Eisenberg and Johnson, 1996).

Parents and teachers are aware that being able to function and thrive in a technological environment will affect a child's future educational and employment opportunities (Roblyer, 2003). An issue currently concerning adults is not if computers should be included in a school's curriculum, but the most effective and appropriate method for incorporating computer technology into a child's educational experience. Adults need to understand approaches for guiding young children's emerging knowledge and interaction with computer hardware and software.

As young children investigate their environment and try to make sense of the world around them, experimentation and interaction with more experienced adults or peers supports a child's growing understanding about their world (Van Hoorn, Monighan Nourot, Scales, & Rodriquez Alward, 2003; Vygotsky, 1978). Young children who are offered opportunities to interact with computers in the home setting might be given assistance from parents or other more knowledgeable individuals. Guidance offered by adults may provide scaffolding for young children, which permits sustained interaction with computers and supports emerging computer knowledge.

STATEMENT OF THE RESEARCH PROBLEM

An Education Resource Information Center (2008) search of computer studies conducted from 1970 to April 2008 revealed 16, 988 studies of computers in education, with 484 studies focusing on computers in early childhood. There have been 58 studies investigating computers and young children in the home which is .003% of the computer studies conducted. There are a mere handful of research studies that have delved into the use of computers by children in the home setting. The need seems palpable for further research to be conducted which focuses on young children interacting with computers in the home. Through research, an understanding may be gained of appropriate approaches for parents, educators, and other adults to support a child's growing understanding of how to interact with computers.

Since the 1970s, researchers have attempted to understand children's interaction with computers. Computer studies that were conducted focused on children using computers in the school setting. Studies examined children's actions and the role of teachers when children were using computers. One of the main purposes of this study was to examine the strategies utilized by adults, which support children's emerging computer knowledge. Strategies might include using verbal language to support learning and offering access to computers.

This descriptive study focuses on the computer activities of 6-year-old children and their parents in the home setting. The word *parent* and the phrase *young children* will be mentioned frequently throughout this research. The researcher puts forth the following definitions to clarify the terms. In the study the term parent refers to a child's biological parent, adoptive parent, or primary caregiver. The term young children refers to children preschool through 8 years of age. Emergence of literacy occurring in the home setting has been researched (Dickinson & Tabors, 2001; Martens, 1996; Storch & Whitehurst, 2001; Taylor, 1983; Teale, 1986) and has enabled a comprehensive understanding of how the process of literacy acquisition occurs. Limited research exists that offers examination of computer activity by children in the home setting (Downes, 1998; Facer, Furlong, Furlong, & Sutherland, 2003; Land, 1999). Just as the emergence of literacy skills by young children has been examined in the home setting, there is a need for research that examines children's emergence of computer literacy skills. By observing parents guiding young children interacting with computers in the home setting, educators and researchers might learn effective strategies for adults to utilize when guiding children's acquisition of computer knowledge in the school setting.

Research Questions

This study examined approaches offered by parents for young children interacting with computers. Research questions considered include:

1. What strategies do these parents utilize to offer their children guidance and access to computers?
2. What language categories and patterns do these parents utilize to guide their young children interacting with computers?
3. What do these parents consider the significance of computers in their children's lives and what are common goals for their children's acquisition of computer knowledge?

THEORETICAL RATIONALE

Social Interaction and Learning

The theories and theorists that have influenced this current study include Vygotsky's sociocultural theory of development, Bandura's social cognitive theory (SCT), and Bronfenbrenner's ecological systems theory. The fundamental commonality of all three theories is that learning occurs for a child with the individual as part of a social setting. For the current study the primary caregivers were the parents of the 6-year-old children learning how to interact with home computers.

Vygotsky

Vygotsky (1978) considered every function in the child's cultural development as appearing twice: first on the social level, and later on the individual level; first occurring between people (interpsychological) and then within the child (intrapsychological). Major concepts of Vygotsky (1978) are the zone of proximal development (ZPD), scaffolding, and the importance of play as a tool for learning.

According to Vygotsky (1978) the acquisition of language is a pivotal occurrence for children in their social learning environment. Language is considered essential as a means for social interaction, as well as self-reflection and thought. The cognitive tool of language allows children to think about the world around them, to problem solve, and to learn by accessing knowledge and exchanging information with experienced individuals in their social environment (Eggen & Kauchak, 2001). A child's developmental achievements for language and learning occur in the context of "close relationships . . . typically with parents or those who serve the parental role in the child's life" (Shonkoff & Phillips, 2000, p. 244). There are many ways in which parents support a young child's growing linguistic and cognitive development (Shonkoff & Phillips, 2000). When parents speak to their children or read details from a computer screen, an adult is acting as a mediator between children and the new information. Language is the tool that enables this transference of knowledge and information.

As young children explore their environment and try to make sense of the world around them, interaction with others as well as the guidance of more experienced adults or peers enables learning to occur (Puckett & Black, 2001; Vygotsky, 1978). ZPD is the level of concept development at which a child is not able to accomplish a task or understand a concept independently, but is able to do so with assistance from an adult or more knowledgeable peer (Vygotsky, 1978). ZPD explains a theory of knowledge acquisition and a theory for how learning could occur in the home environment (Gallagher, 2002). During a child's language development, the ZPD is evident as a toddler's emerging language skills are supported and encouraged through interactions that occur with parents and other adults or more experienced peers in a child's social environment. For example, during social interaction in the home environment, parents interacting with their children at the computer may name parts of the computer and encourage the toddler to repeat the words. Through this supported learning experience, expansion of knowledge occurs.

According to Steward (1995), who based her work on Vygotsky's ZPD, through experimentation, errors, and assistance from an adult, the child will learn to independently say new words; then, scaffolding will be withdrawn and the proximal development for this vocabulary expansion task will have ended. Assistance and support provided by adults or more experienced individuals are necessary when a child is learning new ideas or concepts. When children are engaged in collaborative activities, parents and other adults involved in the child's early learning process often use mediation and guidance for learning that transpires.

At the computer, an adult may assist a child's growing computer knowledge by explaining the functions for parts of a computer and guiding a child who is trying to interact with a computer. During guidance at the computer, an adult can support a child's expansion of new technology-related vocabulary words and acquisition of knowledge of how to use a computer. A task or concept that a child needs assistance with as they are developing an understanding will become part of their mental growth and development once the concept has been mastered. At that time, scaffolding may be withdrawn, as the child is able to independently complete the task or understand a concept.

Through the social interaction of play, a child is able to build language skills, express thoughts, problem solve, and acquire knowledge. Vygotsky considered play as one way of creating a zone of proximal development (Fromberg, 2002). "The social context and manner in which children come to use computers as objects for play determine their comfort level with this aspect of technology in their lives" (Van Hoorn et al., 2003, p. 267). How adults arrange the play environment could influence and direct the play themes children select (Berk & Winsler, 1995). The opportunity to play and try various approaches in understanding how to be able to use computers is important to a child's growing understanding.

Through exploration and discovery, trial and error, and experiencing cause-and-effect relationships, children acquire skills and learn about their world. An adult needs to understand how to provide appropriate scaffolding while a child is exploring and acquiring knowledge. The primary purpose of an adult throughout the learning process is not to impart knowledge to the child but to lead the child to observe and think (Kostelnik, Soderman, & Whiren, 1999). During play at the computer, young learners are striving to construct their own knowledge. Active involvement and guidance of a prepared adult are imperative during the discovery process at the computer.

Vygotsky's (1978) theory of development considers the social interaction of children as maintaining a fundamental role in the development of cognition. Social interaction enables children to test their understandings and acquire a framework for interpreting experiences (Vygotsky, 1978). The epistemology of constructivism offers a possible rationale for how the acquisition of knowledge occurs in young children (Abdal-Haqq, 2001). Constructivism is a perspective "of learning and development that emphasizes the active role of the learner in building understanding and making sense of the world" (Eggen & Kauchak, 2001, p. 60). As young children explore their environment and try to make sense of the world around them, interaction with others and the guidance of adults support understandings that emerge. Some parents or significant adults in a child's environment may be able to provide an arena that facilitates the experimentation and exploration needed for the development of computer knowledge.

According to the social constructivist approach to learning, social interaction and the social environment of the child have the strongest impact on a child's developing cognition (Abdal-Haqq, 2001). The researcher regards a child as an individual within a sociocultural context where the dialectical relationship exists; the child interacts and changes the environment and the environment has an influence on and changes the child. Social constructivists view society and the cultural context that a child is situated in as essential to a child's emerging understanding of the world around the individual. Vygotsky (1978) viewed a child's early learning as occurring when a child is given the opportunity for exploration, experimentation, and manipulation of materials in their environment (Kostelnik et al., 1999; Morrow, 2001).

Vygotsky (1978) viewed learning as socially constructed, where children learn what is necessary to be able to participate within their society and culture through interactions with cultural tools that are mediated by adults or more experienced peers. If a child has perceived adults in the home environment as allies, asking teachers for assistance in the school setting may seem like a possible option to solving questions that arise when using a computer. If the child usually asks a sibling or more experienced friend for assistance at the computer, then working with a partner might be the approach to learning that a child might attempt. The constructivist approach views the child as a social being who, through social life, acquires a framework for interpreting experiences (North Central Regional Educational Laboratory, 2002).

Bandura

Bandura (1986) proposed that children learn not only from direct instruction but also from observing significant individuals in the environment and modeling actions observed. Bandura and Walters (1963) found that children tended to imitate individuals whom they admire, have a positive relationship with, and receive some kind of reward from for the behaviors displayed. According to SCT significant adults in a child's life are important role models for learning and imitation of behavior that young children will exhibit (Bandura, 1986; Puckett & Black, 2001). For the development of cognition and literacy, the role of imitation is relevant as a reinforcing factor by parents for children's behaviors that parents value, and which gradually become self-reinforcing for a child (Puckett & Black, 2001). SCT suggests "behavior, the environment, and personal factors, such as beliefs and expectations, all influence each other" (Eggen & Kauchak, 2001, p. 235). Parents using computers at home for email, educational endeavors, or exploring topics on the Internet are role modeling computer skills and also conveying the value placed on having computer knowledge.

Young children may continually try to understand, interact with, and learn from their immediate environment such as the home setting. Obtaining new knowledge can be supported and guided by adults in the child's immediate environment. Children are dependent on their parents for providing them with much of their early learning (Shonkoff & Phillips, 2000). The social environment occurring when an adult and child work together at a computer allows opportunities for discussion, interaction, and a positive learning experience for both parent and child. Social constructivists view the impact of a child's culture, social environment, and interaction with those around them as being primary for a child's developing cognition (Eggen & Kauchak, 2001). The early experiences a child encounters at home while trying to understand how to use a computer may impact the attitude and aptitude a child brings to the school arena. Does the child enjoy working at the computer? Does the child feel capable with trying to use a computer? Does the child only follow explicit instructions given or experiment when new or different computer task challenges are presented?

Bandura's social cognitive theory also addresses the issue of individuals working independently and understanding abstract information. According to Pajares (2004), a major focus of Bandura's theory addresses the symbolizing capacity of humans:

> By drawing on their symbolic capabilities, people can comprehend their environment, construct guides for action, solve problems cognitively, support forethoughtful courses of action, gain new knowledge by reflective thought, and communicate with others at any distance in time and space. By symbolizing their experiences, people give structure, meaning, and continuity to their lives. (p. 12)

When interacting with the abstract environment of computers children need to decipher information, decide actions to be taken, and utilize reflective thought. Young computer users need to gain an understanding of the computer experience and make sense of the symbolic information presented.

In the sociocultural context of the home, the discourse that occurs at the computer between a parent and child may convey the adult's view of "the computer as a toy and the computer as a tool" (Downes, 1998, p. 282). Does the parent view the computer as an educational tool or as an entertainment machine? Does the parent view computer skills and computer literacy as necessary tools for a child's future academic and workplace success? The importance parents and significant adults place on the need for computer skills and for developing computer literacy will be essential factors impacting a child's exposure to computers and ensuing acquisition of computer knowledge. "Parents convey cultural values and traditions to their children and adjust what they do in light of the attributes they want their children to have" (Shonkoff & Phillips, 2000, p. 259). In American society, the significant adults in a child's immediate environment could influence a child's access or guidance with computers and subsequently have a positive impact on a child's emerging computer knowledge.

Bronfenbrenner

Bronfenbrenner (1989) presented four classifications for his ecological systems theory. The interacting and interdependent systems that a child exists within are the environments that impact "the interactions between and among the systems (that) influence the course of a child's growth, development, and learning" (Puckett & Black, 2001, p.18). The layer closest to the child is known as the microsystem; the environment where and with whom the child spends the major part of time such as home, family, child care provider, or extended family. In the immediate environment of a child the roles of individuals in the system, the relationships that exist, and the experiences that occur, will strongly impact the child (Bronfenbrenner, 1989; Puckett & Black, 2001). The influences of the interrelated systems generate an effect for the child at the center of the microsystem from society inwardly and from the child's world outward (Bronfenbrenner, 1989).

As a child matures and ventures beyond the immediate environment, the impact of the second layer known as the mesosystem occurs. These influences include the child's neighborhood, school, or faith-based organizations. The third layer which impacts a child is the exosystem which consists of factors such as a parent's employment situation, social networks that parents are involved in, and family participation in community organizations (Bronfenbrenner, 1989). The theorist considers a parent's educational level and employment factors which affect the family such as time away from home; length of workday and job demands will impact both the quantity and quality of relationships and types of child-rearing practices that occur within the family. The macrosystem is the fourth layer in ecological systems theory and contains the elements of the culture, customs, and rules of the society a child and family exist within (Bronfenbrenner, 1989; Puckett & Black, 2001).

The intrafamilial activities occurring within the immediate family setting such as the abilities of a young child's primary caregiver, and extrafamilial activities such as a parent's work situation will impact the care, attention, and quality of experiences a young child encounters while learning and growing (Bronfenbrenner, 1989; Puckett & Black, 2001). In understanding how young children learn with computers, the microsystem of the preschool child may be explored for factors and influences in the immediate environment that will affect learning. A primary factor in considering early acquisition of computer skills is where a child routinely spends the most amount of time and if a computer is available in this environment. Who a young child's primary caregiver is and the individual's comfort with computers will impact a child's early computer learning experiences.

Elements of the mesosystem such as libraries with computer access in a child's neighborhood will influence a young child's exposure to computers (Puckett & Black, 2001). A parent's use of computers at work and resulting skills and knowledge, as well as local government resources for children to learn about computers, are possible exosystem influences for young children's exposure to computers. The current macrosystem of American society values computer knowledge and computer literacy as an important skill for citizens to attain (Armstrong & Casement, 2000; United States Department of Education, 1996).

ACQUISITION OF LITERACY SKILLS

The acquisition of emergent skills such as literacy skills or computer skills is the perspective being adapted for this examination of children's acquisition of computer knowledge. Therefore, before discussion of understanding how to use computers and computer literacy begins, an understanding of children's acquisition of literacy skills will be considered. According to Gee (2002) a New Literacy Studies (NLS) perspective is needed to discuss language and literacy which places the skills "in their full array of cognitive, social, cultural, institutional, and historical contexts" (p. 30). The sociocultural practices and social languages being used by parents in the home setting offer opportunities for children's engagement in meaningful practices which allows acquisition of social languages (Gee, 2002). When considering the acquisition of language and literacy, the contextual elements that a child is situated in need to be considered to fully comprehend how literacy skills develop.

Gee (2002) considers discourse as situations in which people learning social languages integrate ways of talking, listening, writing, reading, acting, interacting, believing, valuing, and feeling (and using various objects, symbols, images, tools, and technologies) in the service of enacting meaningful socially situated identities and activities. Using an NLS perspective offers a more comprehensive viewpoint for the consideration of how literacy skills develop. Discourse and social language used by parents with their children in the home setting needs to be considered to understand the impact on language and literacy skills that develop.

Emergence Approach of Skills and Discourse at the Computer

A computer being available in the primary care setting of a home or day care could enable a child to have opportunities to interact with computers from a young age. Interactions could occur as a child was interested in learning about computers with computer skills gradually emerging during opportunities for experimentation and exploration. An adult who responds to a child's questions about computers or offers opportunities for a child to discover how to use software programs is allowing a child to be an active computer literacy learner. For exploring the acquisition of computer knowledge, the emergent approach is a strategy that is dynamic and enables considering how the gradual emergence of skills occurs. This emergent approach to literacy acquisition is the perspective adapted for this study when examining adult guidance for children at the computer and the emergence of computer knowledge in young children (Ba, Tally, & Tsikalas, 2002).

Cazden's (2001) analysis of discourse occurring at the computer considers the influence of computer software programs as part of the dynamics of language and conversation when two individuals are talking during interaction at the computer. Her discourse analysis approach can be used to examine talk of an adult and child at the computer with the discourse elements of initiation (I), discussion (D), response (R), and follow-up (F). The definition of initiation is the person or software program that begins a discussion that starts at the computer. A child, adult, or computer program may start the conversation that occurs at the computer. Discussion is talk that occurs at the computer. Response is a reaction, verbal or nonverbal, that is offered to the discussion that was initiated. Follow-up is an additional comment that is added to a response that is offered at the computer. IDRF discourse analysis considers "the quality and quantity of speaking rights and listening responsibilities" occurring at the computer (Cazden, p. 125). Language used by adults to scaffold children's growing understanding of how to use a computer might be clarified using Cazden's IDRF format to examine discourse occurring at the computer. The impact of language on children's developing computer literacy is an essential element to consider when exploring the emergence of computer knowledge of young children in the home setting.

The theoretical rationale for the current study is principally forged by Vygotsky's (1978) theories for language acquisition and cognitive development, the sociocultural view for acquiring knowledge, the use of scaffolding by adults in guiding young children, and the importance of parents to guide the learning of their children. Gee's (2002) perspective of language and literacy being situated in a social, cultural, and cognitive context for a child within a family is the point of view that is maintained for the current study. How a young child's literacy grows and develops with the guidance of parents in the home setting is influenced by an array of factors that are considered in the current study.

SIGNIFICANCE OF THE STUDY

The current research studies the topic of computer knowledge from an emergent skills perspective. Just as emergent literacy is supported and guided by parents in a young child's life, so can growing knowledge of computers be nourished by significant adults in the immediate environment of a young child. The emergent perspective of the current study is an asset for the research conducted, as an expanding understanding of how to interact with computer hardware and software allows a child to acquire computer skills and computer literacy.

For the current study a mixed method research design was used for the collection and analysis of both qualitative and quantitative data. The use of qualitative and quantitative data offers the collection and integration of different kinds of data that focus on the same phenomenon (Creswell, 2002). The use of qualitative research as a component of the research design for the study allows exploration of a central phenomenon, in this case children and parents using computers, as the researcher seeks to understand participants' experiences (Creswell, 2002; Maxwell, 1996; Merriam, 1998). Choosing a descriptive approach to be able to examine research questions being asked is a strength as the purpose of the study is more open-ended in the quest to learn from participants' experiences. The use of quantitative, descriptive research for the current study enables the researcher to describe attributes of frequencies and percentages when analyzing resulting data (Creswell, 2002; McMillan & Wergin, 2005).

The study examined interaction with computers for young children as occurring in the home setting. The need for research of younger children interacting with computers is prevalent. By exploring how adults guide children when computers are used, an understanding may be gained of how to support a child's emerging computer knowledge. Examining how adults provide guidance and access to computers may add to the current understanding of how to provide optimal environments for young children learning how to use computers.

The significance of this descriptive study in understanding parental perspectives for computer use, strategies adults utilized to guide children at the computer, and the perceived importance of computers by parents for their children will add to the current knowledge of how children learn to use computers. Through the triangulation of data, an essential aspect of the current study will be gaining an understanding of approaches adults use to guide young children at the computer and the impact of strategies used.

A significant aspect of this study is the analysis of language patterns and categories that emerged from the data. The verbal support offered by adults guiding young children at the computer may enable continued computer interaction while also offering information for understanding how to utilize computer hardware and software. Parents assist a young child's acquisition of knowledge and cognitive expansion through the use of language as a tool for learning. The strength of the current study is the use of discourse analysis to understand strategies adults use with children that enables sustained interaction when children are engaged with using computer hardware and software.

The significance of the study researching adult language categories used in the home setting could be used as a base for future research of adult language at the computer. Examining the language category results of parents could be compared to categories and patterns used by early childhood educators guiding young children in school settings. Comparisons of the different contextual environments with differences in quantity of adult discourse categories may offer information that could benefit educational strategies.

LIMITATIONS OF THE STUDY

The current mixed methods research uses a case study approach, which may be a limitation when attempting to investigate the open-ended and broad research questions posed. The collection of information from a small number of participants may be a limiting factor of the study (Creswell, 2002; Merriam, 1998). One of the limitations for this mixed methods study is that only six children interacting with computers will be included in the research. The small sample size restricts the generalizations that can be presented for other populations of young children.

In the future a larger sample of young children from different socioeconomic backgrounds, with various family dynamic groupings, would need to be examined. Following different populations of children's use in a variety of settings would expand on information gained. The current study focused on English-speaking American children. Future studies could focus on non-English-speaking children or English-speaking American children whose parents are bilingual. Settings that could be used for observations of children and adults interacting at the computer are school environments, friends' homes, after-school programs, library settings, or parents' workplaces.

Another limitation of the study is that the home computer was not considered within the dynamics of the entire family structure. Family members may vie for use of the home computer, may interact at the computer, or may interact through the computer; these aspects of computer activity affect resulting computer experiences. The computer as part of the home environment and the interaction that occurs among family members through the technology would offer a fuller portrait of the influence of home computers on family dynamics.

The current study focused solely on computer activity in the home setting. The computer is one technology activity in a household along with other technologies such as video games, portable media players such as iPods, and other technology choices. To gain a fuller understanding of how computers are used and are part of family dynamics, the integrated use of a family computer needs to be examined within the context of family member technology usage. Therefore, a limitation of the current study is the focus solely on the computer for technological usage in the home setting.

Another limitation of the study is the brief time frame in which the observations were conducted. Considering computer use by young children in the home setting, over a period of time, would require a longitudinal study to be conducted. Long-term studies may offer an understanding of the dynamics occurring when computers are available and used over a period of time. The results could allow a researcher to offer inferences about development of skills for the same subjects at different points in time (Tuckman, 1999).

Longitudinal studies have been conducted in the school setting, such as the 10-year study conducted at Florida State University examining the use of computers in the classroom for children from kindergarten through sixth grade (Butzin, 2002). Future research could consider the use of a longitudinal study in the home setting, which would follow the development of computer awareness and emerging understandings. Limitations of the study offer possibilities for future research but do not limit the significance of the current information gained.

Computers are an integral element in American society today. Parents and teachers seek to prepare children to be productive adults who are able to successfully thrive in the technological world of computers. The current study seeks to expand on present research in attempting to understand the parents' role as mediator for children's developing computer knowledge.

2   Review of Related Research and Literature

The current study examined the strategies and approaches utilized by parents guiding young children at the computer in the home setting. Language used by parents when interacting with their children at the computer was considered. Parental perspectives for the significance of computers in the lives of their children and goals for development of computer knowledge were also examined. The review of related research and literature will begin with a discussion of how researchers view the impact of new technologies on children. Next research studies will be reviewed that focused on children using computers in school settings. Recent studies, which research computers in the home setting, will be examined in detail. Through the review of related research and literature, a perspective will be offered for the current research and a rationale for research that is needed.

HISTORY OF TECHNOLOGY AND RESEARCH

Researchers have examined the use and impact of technology on children from the introduction of movies in the early 1900s, to the beginnings of radio in the 1930s, to television and American culture of the 1950s and 1960s, and for children and computers from the late 1970s until now (Armstrong & Casement, 2000; Wartella & Jennings, 2000). Research for each of the technologies such as film, radio, television, and computers has followed similar recurrent patterns for each new technology. Proponents consider the educational benefits and positive influence on the child, while opponents ponder the destructive possibilities and negative impact on the developing child (Wartella & Jennings, 2000).

Wartella and Jennings (2000) noted that with each new technology, researchers initially consider the demographics and utilization by children. Initial studies for the movies focused on which children were attending movies and the movies these children went to in the 1920s and 1930s. For radio, studies considered which children had access to radios and the radio shows children listened to in the 1930s and 1940s. The effect of the radio on children's other activities such as reading and school studies were examined. In the 1950s and 1960s which children had access to televisions and the television shows children were viewing were analyzed. The effect of television on social activities, academic endeavors, and attitudes of children were also considered (Wartella & Jennings, 2000). For computers, researchers initially deliberated children's access to computers in school, amount of time spent on computers, software selected for use, and the influence on other social and educational activity choices (Wartella & Reeves, 1983).

With each of the media technologies, studies by researchers turned from the initial topics of children's time and preference with the technology, to the issue of the content of the technology. For movies, radio, and television the results of the information by researchers was used as fuel by advocacy groups to take steps to prevent what was viewed as the demoralization and corruption of children (Wartella & Jennings, 2000). Parents and religious groups called for government intervention and regulation. Censorship and guidelines were created for each media of the movies, radio, and television to try to prevent the "vulgarization of American culture" (Armstrong & Casement, 2000, p. 16).

The lessons that can be learned from previous media research studies can be a positive guide for the issue of children and computers. "New partnerships between academics, content providers, and government are needed to create new incentives for developing higher-quality media that builds on what has been learned about media effects on children" (Wartella & Jennings, 2000, p. 39). Research with computers is progressing past the initial studies phase of analyzing the demographic or utilization patterns of children and is beginning to focus on finding ways that the technology is able to have a positive impact on children interacting with the media.

Computer Research in the School Setting

During the 1970s computers had become part of the environment for scientific research, industry, and the business world. In the late 1970s computers began to be included in some school settings predominantly for skill-and-drill activities (Armstrong & Casement, 2000). In the late 1970s researchers and educators debated whether computers were here to stay in American society and in particular for educational purposes. The research response was that computers would grow and expand as part of American culture and educational environments (Papert, 1993).

Initial research with computers in education was presented from two approaches: computers for educational reinforcement such as skill-and-drill and teaching children to learn computer programming (Papert, 1980). Computer software practice programs offering remedial reinforcement began with high school students and for students with developmental disabilities (Armstrong & Casement, 2000). Teaching children from kindergarten through high school the computer language of BASIC became a widespread practice in schools during the late 1970s and early 1980s (Armstrong & Casement, 2000). Seymour Papert (1980) was the lead researcher for a Massachusetts Institute of Technology (MIT) team of artificial intelligence researchers who developed a children's version of computer programming language known as Logo. The use of computer language geared to younger children caused the widespread inclusion of programming in elementary schools (Armstrong & Casement, 2000).

Papert (1993) considered himself an educational utopian because he believed that "very powerful computational technology and computational ideas can provide children with new possibilities for thinking, learning, and growing emotionally as well as cognitively" (pp. 17–18). He wanted to encourage educators to guide children to think about thinking as well as to learn about learning through the use of Logoprogramming. Papert's research of the 1970s and 1980s viewed computers as a tool that would become an integral part of American society. Papert predicted "a future where a computer will be part of every child's life" (p. 18). He foresaw the price of personal computers dropping to be reasonable enough for massive numbers of individuals to purchase personal computers.

Papert (1993) did accurately predict what would come to pass for the massive inclusion of computers in American society. The utilization of Logo continued through the 1980s but did not end educators' use of computers for skill-and-drill (Armstrong & Casement, 2000). The creation of word processing programs and the development of CD-ROMs during the late 1980s, as well as the expansion of the Internet during the 1990s, has caused researchers and educators to reevaluate the use of computers as an educational tool in schools.

Becker (1985) conducted a national survey to find out how schools were using computers. In 1983, he reported that 250,000 computers were available in schools for 45 million students. Government reports such as *A Nation at Risk* (National Commission on Excellence in Education, 1983) called for educational reform and action to ensure future economic and global strength for America. The report stressed the argument that "the United States will fall behind in international stature if the young are not appropriately trained, and this means training for the postindustrial, knowledge-based society" (p. 52). The *Nation at Risk* report and Becker's survey enabled the government and schools to realize that action had to be taken in order for more children to learn using computers in the school setting.

As computers became part of the educational environment at the high school level, researchers contemplated "Even if we cannot say that microcomputers have been fully integrated into secondary education yet, we can ask whether they are here to stay or just another fad" (Rogers, McManus, Peters, & Kim, 1985, p. 159). *A Nation at Risk* deemed the necessity for computers to be part of every student's learning experience. Educators began to realize that computers were the wave of the future and were becoming an interminable part of the educational arena. During the early 1980s the main uses for computers in education were most often for drill and practice activities and to teach programming skills to students (Becker, 1983).

For researchers focusing on children and computers, in the mid-1980s the educational debate turned to whether it was appropriate to use computers with younger children (Davidson, 1989). Clements (1985) suggested that even among preschoolers, the computer might challenge and alter traditional instructional modes. A valid perspective from Davidson about the lack of research for young children and computers was offered by the observation that in preschools the value of most materials used has been verified by research. During the 1980s the possible perceived hazards of computer use by young children included computers being socially isolating, computer activities being too abstract, computers replacing other childhood experiences, and computers forcing children to learn skills before developmentally ready to do so (Haugland & Wright, 1997).

In the 1990s research and debate of children with computers continued to focus on both the benefits and possible hazards of children using computer technology. The National Center for Education Statistics (NCES, 2001) reported that in the 1990s research of computers in schools and classrooms had focused primarily on availability of educational technology. Muffoletto and Knupfer (1993) suggested that as schools are told they must enter the Information Age the typical history on computer technology narrows the discussion to the chronological developments of hardware and acquisition of hardware by educators. The Technology Literacy Challenge (United States Department of Education, 1996) offered federal funding to support educational endeavors for integration of computers and educational technology into all school curriculums in the United States. The pressure which began in the 1980s for schools to prepare students for the Information Age continued into the 1990s with computers (as part of educational technology) being a major focus of reform and policy at the local, state, and federal levels (NCES, 2001).

According to Liang and Johnson (1999) in the 1990s, most schools, teachers, and students still used computers only as the equivalent of expensive flash cards or electronic worksheets. In the early 1990s in elementary schools the primary use of computers continued to be for drill and practice purposes (NCES, 2001). There was beginning to be a decline by some educators in using computers to teach programming and an emergence of computers as a tool for learning content (Becker, 1994; Sutton, 1991). Liang and Johnson (1999) considered the use of computers to introduce new skills and concepts as insufficient because young children were thought to need concrete experiences to learn about the world around them. During the mid- to late-1990s, researchers began to focus on the use of computers by young children in educational settings (Clements, 1998; Elkind, 1998).

In the late 1990s the NCES (2001) noted, "School computer use had shifted to some degree to reflect a greater emphasis on problem solving and in-depth learning and less emphasis on drill and practice and basic skills" (p. 2). Computers were in computer laboratories and classrooms, and were becoming part of daily activity in schools (Armstrong & Casement, 2000). The need to be proficient with computers is still touted by schools as an essential that is required for children to succeed in the future workforce and for the economic success of America in the global economy (Armstrong & Casement, 2000; Bitter & Pierson, 2002). *The Enhancing Education Through Technology Act of 2001* (United States Department of Education, 2002) stated that "preparing our children for a lifetime of computer use is now just as essential as teaching them to read and write and do math" (p. 2).

The use of computers in school settings was briefly reported by the National Reading Panel (NRP) in April 2000 with evidence based findings for 21 research studies using computers for reading instruction. The use of computers for reading instruction was examined as a tool to deliver instruction (p. 17). The NRP considers the use of computer word processing software to enhance the effectiveness of combining reading and writing instruction as a trend that is showing promise (p. 18).

Statistics collected by the United States Census Bureau (2003) reflect the increasing pattern of computer use in schools. In 1993, 59% of children in elementary and secondary schools were using computers in the school setting. By 1997, the percentage had increased to 70.4%. In 2003 the total of elementary and secondary students using computers in the school setting was 83.5%. In 2003, for children under age 5, 42.6% were using computers in the school setting and for children ages 5–9 the percentage using computers was 80.1%. In 2008 schools in the United States claim 100% access to computers in the school setting (Evans, 2007). The availability and quantity of computers in the school setting has increased and the issue has now become the quality and integration of computers as part of children's educational experiences.

Technology and the Government

The United States government has proclaimed the need for Americans to stay current with knowledge that is needed to maintain a quality existence in our society. As stated in *A Nation at Risk* (National Commission on Excellence in Education, 1983):

> The people of the United States need to know that individuals in our society who do not possess the levels of skill, literacy and training essential to this new era will be effectively disenfranchised, not simply from the material rewards that accompany competent performance, but also from the chance to participate fully in our national life. (p. 2)

Educational reform with technology was not tackled by the government until George W. Bush addressed the issue with the *No Child Left Behind Act of 2001* (NCLB) (P.L. 107–110). In January 2002 President Bush initiated educational reform to ensure that the nation's neediest children were not left behind educationally. The President developed a plan to try to improve the performance of America's elementary and secondary schools while at the same time ensuring that no child would be trapped in a failing school.

The NCLB Act of 2001 (P.L. 107–110) incorporates the principles and strategies proposed by the President which included increased accountability for states, school districts, and schools, as well as greater choice for parents and students, particularly those attending low-performing schools. The NCLB Act includes a technology section entitled Enhancing Education Through Technology (EETT) which had offered federal support for expanding computer use in the school setting. The EETT program attempted to improve student academic achievement in elementary and secondary schools through the use of technology. The technology program was an effort to ensure that teachers would integrate technology into the curriculum to improve students' achievement (United States Department of Education, 2002).

Through technology grant programs, states were offered funding to help improve student academic achievement through the use of computers and technology as educational tools (United States Department of Education, 2002). In recent years funding available through the National Education Technology Plan (United States Department of Education, 2005) has been inadequate to enable schools to have current, as well as adequate computers and technology resources in schools to increase opportunities for all students throughout the United States.

A revised National Education Technology Plan (United States Department of Education, 2005) presented in January 2005 imposed new standards of accountability and provided increased flexibility and funding for public schools. One of the goals of the National Education Technology Plan (United States Department of Education, 2005) is for students to be technologically literate by eighth grade. The National Education Technology Plan (2005) states by 1999, 97% of kindergartners had access to a computer at school or home, with 72% of all first graders using home computers during the summer on a weekly basis, and over 85% of young children with home computers using them for educational purposes. The federal government has supported technology planning by offering funding to public schools. The goal of the government is to bring exposure to technology for all American children, allow children opportunities to learn using computers, and for children to be prepared for future school and employment prospects.

Research in Early Childhood Settings

Technology in Early Childhood Classrooms

In the late 1990s early childhood educators began to realize that computers could be part of a nursery school curriculum (Clements, 1998). In 1996 the National Association for the Education of Young Children (NAEYC) stated

"Technology plays a significant role in all aspects of American life today and this role will only increase in the future" (p. 11). The NAEYC (1996) Technology Position Statement is offered to guide teachers and parents in the integration of computers into early childhood education. According to the NAEYC position statement for technology and young children "the appropriate and beneficial use of technology with young children is ultimately the responsibility of the early childhood educator, working in collaboration with parents" (p. 6). NAEYC has suggested guidelines for inclusion of computers into early childhood programs. The educational debate continues regarding the appropriateness of using computers with young children in the school setting. Further research will assist in clarifying both perspectives of the debate.

To attempt to understand how young children play at the computer in an early childhood classroom, Chang, Rossini, and Pan (1997) posted a question on an early childhood Listserv web site. The aim of the query presented was to find out at what age young children begin to interact with computers and viewpoints of appropriate approaches that should be utilized for young children to interact with computers. Responses to the question posed indicated that children as young as 6 months of age were using computers with their parents while most children began at ages 3 or 4. The viewpoint of some early childhood educators was that the computer is an appropriate tool to enrich teaching and learning (p. 1339). Other educators consider the computer an inappropriate tool because young children should be engaged in experiences with concrete materials and activities.

The research results of Chang et al. (1997) states that when young children are given freedom to explore computers, a positive attitude toward the technology is able to develop. Gaining a positive perspective at a young age might result in children being primed to learn more complex uses of the computer when older. If young children encounter computers as another part of their home environment will the computer then be considered another educational tool by children interacting with the technology? In the current study parent interviews and site observations were used to address questions and results offered by Chang et al. (1997). At what age do young children begin to interact with computers and are computers another educational tool in the home setting? These questions were asked of parents to comprehend their perspective through responses to interview questions and by actions observed as parents guided their children at home computers.

Computers and Literacy

At times a three-way intersection of technology, literacy, and play occurs in early childhood education (Liang & Johnson, 1999). As stated in Liang and Johnson (1999), research conducted by Escobedo (1992), Silvern (1998), and Wright and Shade (1994) was presented, which focused on play and computers with the issue of using computers as elevated tools of play and learning in educational settings. Parents are considered a child's first teacher, therefore children need to be able to play and learn with computers using developmentally appropriate activities (Liang & Johnson, p. 57). An area of concern Liang and Johnson discussed is that teachers need to remember that the use of computers and technology should not be an end to learning but rather an alternate route to learning. According to Liang and Johnson, further exploration is needed at a descriptive level to understand how technology can facilitate or even improve upon emergent literacy and play while avoiding interfering with the established synergism in early childhood education. The current research aligns with Silvern's (1998) view of parents as a child's first teacher. This study seeks to offer further study at a descriptive level of technology, in particular of young children and computers.

Computer Studies in the Home Setting

Research of children using computers has been predominantly focused on activities that occur in school settings. Few studies have examined the use of computers in the home setting. One study that examined computers in the home setting was conducted by Land (1999) and explored the use of computers in homes by children ages 9 to 14. This study used a multimodal and multiphase approach to research children's computer use and influences on computer use in the home. The factors influencing computer use and online use for children in the home setting examined by Land were the demographics of children who use computers, how these children were using computers, the influences on computer use, the use of other media by children, and parent knowledge about their children's computer use (p. 1). The project was implemented in two phases with Phase I being the pilot study for the project. Phase I employed a qualitative approach using observations of seven children ages 8 to 11. Long surveys of the children and their parents were conducted to learn how computers were being used in the home. Phase II used results from the long surveys of Phase I to create two written surveys for children ages 9 to 14 and their parents.

During Phase I researchers obtained permission from parents for home visits to observe their children's home computer interactions. Participants were seven children from middle-class homes in Middle Georgia, age 8 to 11, with families having at least one computer in the home. Visits were arranged and researchers observed children's interaction at a home computer. Site visits lasted between 30 to 60 minutes. During the first site visit an observation sheet was kept to record the type of computer being used, software available and favored, as well as the location of the home computer. Choice and length of computer activities were noted (Land, 1999, pp. 48–49). After observation of the child at the computer concluded, the researcher conducted an interview with the child. A second visit was scheduled with the same families for long interviews to be conducted with one parent.

In Phase II participants were 282 children in fifth to eighth grade and their parents with families having at least one computer in the home. The children attended schools located in Nassau County, Florida, and Baldwin County, Georgia. The Children's In-Home Media Use Survey (Land, 1999) was dispensed in classrooms with children in fifth to eighth grade. The variables considered by questions asked in the child surveys were number of days a week the computer was used and the amount of time the child spent on the computer each day the computer was used. Demographics about the child, other media the child used, experiences with the computer that the child had, and the child's perception of computers and using computers were considered.

Children who had completed the child surveys then brought home the parent/guardian survey, A Survey of Children's In-Home Media Use (Land, 1999). Parents were asked to estimate the number of days and amount of time each day that the child used the home computer. The demographics of parents and families were appraised on parent surveys including marital status, income level, and parents' educational level. Family factors considered in the parent surveys were the child's access to computers, parent use of the home computer, and parent encouragement and guidelines for use of the home computer (p. 86). For parent surveys, 82% were completed by females; 86% of the parents were married; 86.8% of the parents completing surveys were White, 11.4% African American, 4% Hispanic, and 1.4% Asian.

Land's (1999) study concluded that influences on children using their home computer were parental attitude toward computers, children's perceptions of the computer for entertainment and education, the gender of the child, how many computers were in the home, and how many family members were living in a household. Parental control was only an issue when a member of the household needed access to the computer with work, schoolwork, and educational needs taking precedence over entertainment. Over 90% of the parent survey responses consider the computer as "important for their child's future and education" (p. 158).

The current study considered children and computers in the home setting as Land (1999) did with children being 6 years of age. Observations of children interacting with computers in the home setting were used. Land chose one 30–60 minute observation of a child using a home computer. For the current study the researcher visited homes four times with observations ranging from 30–120 minutes. Instead of observations being transcribed from handwritten notes, activity was videotaped. The resulting recordings of the site visits were transcribed and information transferred to a coding sheet. This instrument will be discussed further in Chapter 3. Notes taken during the site visits supplemented the information collected during observations. As in Land's study, long interviews were utilized with one parent from each family. Parental perspectives were examined to consider the importance of computers for their children's educational and future achievement. Parent interviews and observations during home visits will corroborate parent views on this issue. The data collection and analysis offered by Land's study provided a source of possibilities for design and rationale of the current study.

Home Computer Use

Downes (1998) completed a study that was prompted by the researcher's own discussion with education graduate students about how their elementary students' computer use at school might compare to use at home. The study focused on development of an understanding of the "reciprocal relationship between the child and the computer within the sociocultural context of the home" (p. xiii). Downes' perspective of the child encompassed theories from psychological, sociological, and technological perspectives (p. 18). The sociological view considers children in contemporary society within a mesosystem and exosystem, with computers being used for education and entertainment; as a tool for the future, a hobby, and as a productive tool.

The project was conducted in three stages with Stage One focused on the use of computers in the home setting (Downes, 1998). In all stages of the study, a criterion for the children selected for participation was that they had a computer in one of their primary home settings such as their own home or their nonresidential parent's home (p. 141). For Stage One, two researchers worked together to interview 219 children age 5 to 12 at their schools in Sydney, Australia. For group interviews, one researcher was the interviewer and one researcher videotaped discussion that occurred during the group interview activity. Each discussion group had approximately six children with a blend of both boys and girls in each group. Interview sessions lasted between 20 to 40 minutes and were conducted over a three to four day period.

In Stage Two, interviews were conducted with 276 children age 8 to 12 from schools in Sydney, Australia. Researchers interviewed children one-on-one with responses recorded on an interview form and audiotaped to check for accuracy. The third stage delved further into the views of 14 children age 10 to 11, as well as their parents and teachers. The focus of this stage was on the children's use of computer technology. During Stage Three, children kept computer log diaries and were interviewed. Parents and teachers were also interviewed and all interviews were audiotaped (Downes, 1998).

In Stage Three, Downes' (1998) tape-recorded interviews of children, parents, and teachers were transcribed. The transcriptions were then sent to the adults interviewed to ensure that their ideas and views were accurately conveyed or if they wanted to add additional information. Children's transcribed interviews from Stage Two and Stage Three, along with computer diaries, were used to create a composite picture of each child. Children's transcriptions were analyzed "for common themes and differences in approaches to computing" (p. 136). Parent transcriptions were analyzed "for elaboration of existing themes from previous stages or emerging themes that specifically related to the families' social and cultural context, as well as beliefs of the parents about computing at home and at school" (p. 136).

The major findings of the study revealed that the resources available to the children were similar in a broad sense for the hardware and software in their homes. The children could play games using a range of software, draw, and use word processing programs. The differences in family incomes influenced whether the computers had CD-ROMs and printers (Downes, 1998). According to the findings, from the sociocultural perspective the children used their home computers as a tool and as a toy. Parents did convey strong beliefs in the computer as a tool for future success for their children.

A significant contribution of Downes' (1998) study is in gaining an understanding of the child and computer being in a reciprocal relationship, with both maintaining "the roles of actor and being acted upon . . . (which) highlights the importance of the sociocultural context within which the interactions between child and computer take place" (p. 295). The impact of how children use computers in their home setting needs to be understood for adults to be prepared to guide children appropriately in the home or school setting.

The use of videotaping and then transcription of the recordings was utilized by Downes (1998) to explore common themes and differences in approaches to using computers. Downes considered parental descriptors of parent workplace computer use, parental home computer use, and computer use by gender which the current research will take into consideration. Downes used multiple sources of data in trying to understand how computers are being used in the home setting and this is applicable to the current study.

The current study drew on the same theoretical rationale as Downes' (1998) study considering the child as being embedded sociologically within a family unit. Parents guiding their children are integrated within the same contextual environment. Downes studied children ranging in age from 8 to 12 while the current study will have children age 6 as participants. Both studies consider parental perspectives when trying to understand children's use of computers in the home setting. Downes' doctoral study included the use of discussion groups, semi-structured and structured interviews, and children's self-reporting computer-use diaries (p. 115). Downes employed the multimethod approach and multiple sources of data necessary in order to gain an understanding of how the computer was being used in the home setting. Triangulation was accomplished by the use of the multimethod approach, multiple sources of data collection, and the use of multiple researchers as strategies to augment internal validity (pp. 114–115). The current study will employ triangulation of sources and the multimethod approach for data collection.

Case Study Approach

Facer et al. (2003) studied computers in the home and considered the significance of technology as being affected by "the existing values, practices, and interests of the family itself" (p. 5). The case study approach reflected the use of computers with children in both the home and school setting.

The project was conducted in three phases from 1998 until October 2000 with locations in England and Wales. Eighteen case study children and their families were selected to include a sampling of children from different background factors that might impact computer use (p. 11).

In Phase I written questionnaires were completed by 855 children ages 9 to 10 and 13 to 14 in four sites in the south of Wales and southwest England. The comprehensive questionnaires focused on home and school use of computers. Case studies which focused on the use of home computers were conducted over an 18-month period for 18 children age 9 to 12. The second phase included interviews that were conducted with case study children, their parents and siblings, teachers, and friends. Observations of the 18 children's computer use were also part of Phase II. For Phase III, a group interview was conducted for 48 children who had responded to study questionnaires and considered themselves as low computer users (Facer et al., 2003).

The results of data collected offered descriptive information about children as computer users and their families, tally counts and percentages for information about computers, computer use and the impact on children and their families. Facer et al. (2003) conducted surveys on children's computer use in June 1998; June 2000; June, September, and October 2001. Descriptive information tables for locations of case study families' home computers, listing children's names and computer locations were offered. The descriptive information proposes that "in order to understand family negotiations around computers, we need to recognize that computers are often (a) *shared resource* within homes" (p. 47). For surveys conducted, 6% of children had exclusive access to their own computer, 53% from one survey and 64% from another survey used a home computer located in common family space (pp. 47–48).

The home setting afforded case study children time and opportunity to choose and engage in interaction with activities which the children had selected. The results of the Facer et al. (2003) study is in agreement with Downes' (1998) study that during game play on a home computer, exploratory learning surfaces and children learn by doing (p. 189). The study found that in the home setting the ways that the case study children learned from and with other people appeared to be an apprenticeship model for learning (p. 191). Instead of a novice and expert dyad, in the home setting learning, "often involved a more cooperative enterprise in which both parent and child were co-constructing knowledge" (p. 192).

The Facer et al. (2003) study conclusion that in the home setting children learn from people through an apprenticeship model is an important finding to consider for the current study. Will parents participating in the current study be offering an apprenticeship model for their children when they interact at the computer in the home setting? Is the cooperative enterprise that Facer et al. found with parents and children co-constructing knowledge in operation as parents and children interact at the home computer? There are elements of the Facer et al. study that were replicated in the current research including the use of a case study approach, the home setting being considered as a key site for understanding computer use, and the use of a family information chart to summarize the features of families participating in the current study.

Home Computer Access

There are various family dynamics that affect whether or not a young child is able to interact with a home computer such as the number of family members living in the household, if parents are married or divorced, the jobs parents have, the number of hours parents work each week, the resulting influence of work on the time a parent is available at home, as well as the number, age, and gender of siblings. These dynamics will influence the quality and quantity of possible computer resources parents might be able to provide for children in a home setting. In one household there may be more than one home computer available for use by family members. In another household, having one computer for the family may be a nonessential luxury that is not feasible to purchase.

The functionality of a home computer will influence what a child is able to learn during computer use. According to Becker (2000), full functionality of a computer is when the unit has the features of "a hard disk drive, a CD-ROM drive, a printer, a modem, and a mouse or similar pointing device" (p. 63). For children the second strongest predictor of computer use is having a fully functional computer (Becker, 2000). Having a computer that operates properly with a wide selection of software options is more enticing to a child trying to interact with a home computer. Allowing a child to use a home computer, having a computer that is fully functional, and providing resources to keep the computer operational are important ways that parents are able to support a child's growing understanding of how to use a computer. Research studies have examined the role and possible positive or negative impact that family resources offer for children learning to use computers (Armstrong & Casement, 2000; Becker, 2000; Shonkoff & Phillips, 2000). Family resources may impact parents' ability to provide young children with access to a computer in the home setting.

Adults Scaffolding Children's Learning Experiences

The role of supportive adults scaffolding young children's learning has been examined by Coltman, Petyaeva, and Anghileri (2002) for aspects of 3-D shape and mathematical concepts. Although the research study focused on learning mathematical skills, the relevance for children learning with adult guidance is pertinent to the current study of parents guiding children at the home computer. The Coltman et al. (2002) research study was framed by Vygotsky's (1978) "cultural historical theory" (p. 40). In the study, key considerations were the design of playful contexts for the activities that would be used and adult interactions (Coltman et al., 2002, p. 40). The social constructivist theory as described by Pollard and Tann (1993) in Coltman et al. (2002) is a form of constructivism "which strongly suggests the importance for learning of the social context and of interaction with others" (p. 124). An adult working as a guide with a child would be able to assist while the child is engaged in an activity "followed by support and instruction and a cycle is established which takes learning forward beyond the level which the child would have reached alone" (p. 41).

When children manipulate play materials independently, they may "serendipitously solve a particular problem without being aware of the relationship between their actions and the solution . . . hence they would be unable to transfer their method to new situations or another task" (Coltman et al., 2002, p. 41). When an adult is involved in the child's interaction with materials, the child is able to be made aware of the implications for the actions taken in being able to accomplish a task. Coltman et al. state that with an adult's assistance "the child is aware not only of the found solution, but of the processes which led to its discovery" (p. 41).

The Coltman et al. (2002) study uses Bruner's (1990) model of scaffolding as a "form of intervention in which the adult and child establish a 'co-construction' of meaning through a system of graded help" (p. 42). The study focused on the impact of adult support on children's learning for children attempting to problem solve tasks, which are embedded in playful contexts. Study results confirmed that for certain learning experiences, in this case aspects of space and shape, children may not be able to discover the required knowledge and approaches to solving tasks solely by independent manipulation of materials. Adults or other experienced individuals may be able to provide children with graded levels of adult guidance, which will significantly improve the efficacy of learning certain tasks.

For parents and educators, it is important to understand the relevance of scaffolding for certain tasks, as young children will "learn these (tasks) more effectively through carefully structured joint activity with *experienced others*" (Coltman et al., 2002, p. 48). The importance of scaffolding is a key factor in selecting parents as the focal point in the current study and considering how they offer their children guidance with computers in the home setting.

SUMMARY OF REVIEW OF LITERATURE

The studies reviewed offered commonalities, as well as unique aspects for research that has been conducted with computers. The research studies examined were all focused on children and computers (Chang et al., 1997; Coltman et al. 2002; Downes, 1998; Facer et al., 2003; Land, 1999; Liang & Johnson, 1999; Lumpkins, Ryborn, Herrin, & Parker, 1995). The ages varied from preschool through teenagers but all the studies explored how children interact with computers.

When research on children interacting with computers began, the research setting was primarily in schools and predominantly focused on children's independent interactions with computers. In the late 1990s children and computers in the home setting began to be explored and focused on the impact and use of computers by children (Downes, 1998; Land, 1999). Facer et al. (2003) conducted a case study approach for a study to explore how young people were making use of computers in the home setting. The home setting was the focus of Land's (1999) research that utilized surveys and long interviews with parents to understand the influences of computer use in the home (p. 1).

Understanding parental perspectives about the importance and impact of computers for their children has been explored in recent research studies (Downes, 1998; Facer et al., 2003; Land, 1999). Although Downes utilized audiotaping when interviewing parents, videotaping was used when children were interviewed in groups. Lumpkins et al. (1995) used written surveys to gain an understanding of parent perspectives on the use of computers by their children. In the studies reviewed the effect of parents' attitudes on a child's use and access to computers, explored by Downes (1998), Facer et al. (2003), and Land (1999), was considered a focal point for the current study.

Through research and assessment of parents interacting with young children during home computer use, an understanding may be gained of how parents guide young children, offer children access to computers, and how parents perceive, interact with, and assist children with learning to use computers. There is a paucity of research focused on young children being guided when interacting with computers in the home setting. The review of literature has reinforced the need for the current study of parents guiding 6-year-old children's emerging computer knowledge and interaction with computers in the home setting. The research which focused on adults interacting with children at the computer has mainly been explored in the school setting. As with other emergent literacies, the need to understand learning in the home environment will impact approaches used in educational settings. The current study focused on parent guidance of their young children interacting with computers in the home setting.

3   Research Study

In today's society, "the public generally agrees that for children to participate socially, economically, and politically in this new and different world,
they must acquire a certain level of comfort and competence in using computers" (Shields & Behrman, 2000, p. 5). The number of parents providing
their children with access to computers in the home setting has increased
and "among households with children ages 2 to 17, home computer ownership jumped from 48% in 1996 to 70% in 2000" (p. 5).

Exploring approaches parents use to guide young children's interaction and emerging knowledge when using computers in the home setting
is essential to understand. Just as parents guide children as literacy skills
emerge, adults need to understand approaches that could be utilized when
guiding young children's emerging computer knowledge. The feasibility
study is also discussed in this chapter. The chapter is divided into sections
to describe the research design, research setting, participants, instruments,
procedures, and data analysis that were used for this research study.

PARTICIPANTS, MATERIALS, AND PROCEDURES

Qualitative/Quantitative Research Study Design

The research design for this study gleaned design factors from relevant studies that have examined the use of computers by children (Downes, 1998;
Facer et al., 2003; Land, 1999). The resulting research design required the
use of both qualitative and quantitative methodology for collection and
analysis of data. Therefore the study design utilizes a qualitative/quantita-
tive design for the current study (Creswell, 2002).

Qualitative research utilizes data collection methodology that seeks to
explore social phenomena in its naturally occurring contexts, without the
existence of predetermined assumptions or categories, and allows for in-
depth exploration of this environment and experience (Bogden & Biklen,
1992). Qualitative research design takes place in the natural setting where
the event being observed occurs with the researcher as an instrument of

data collection. In the current study quantitative analysis of data from the parent interviews and review of transcriptions resulted in frequency counts and percentages (Creswell, 2002; McMillan & Wergin, 2005).

Case study is a type of qualitative research design in which the researcher provides an in-depth exploration of an activity, event, or process based on extensive data collection (Creswell, 2002). Merriam (1998) views the use of case study design in qualitative research as being employed "to gain an in-depth understanding of the situation and meaning for those involved" (p. 19). For the current research considering interactions between parents and children in the home setting, a case study design augmented the quality of data collected during site visits. The interest in the process of parent-child interactions that occur at the computer in the home setting was addressed by the case study approach.

Research Setting

The research setting for the current study was based on the setting of the feasibility study which was conducted with families residing in Staten Island, New York. Staten Island is one of five boroughs that comprise New York City. Staten Island is considered an urban setting. According to the Staten Island Census Statistics (2005) Staten Island has a population of 443,728. The population consists mainly of 77.6% White non-Hispanics, 12.5% Hispanics, and 9.7% Black or African Americans. In 1999 the median income of households was $55,039. For Staten Island individuals age 25 or older, 82.6% have graduated from high school and 24.4% have a bachelor's degree or higher (Staten Island Census Statistics, 2005).

The home setting of six families residing in Staten Island, New York, was the research setting for the current study. The families owned and lived in private single-family homes. Five of the homes were detached and one was attached. In the home setting of the six families, the researcher conducted parent interviews and observed activity at the computer. The research setting of the home enabled the researcher to focus on research question one: What strategies do adults utilize to offer children guidance and access to computers?

Participants

The participant profile for the current study was six 6-year-old children and their parents. For study participation the families had to have a computer available in the home. Families where a parent was available in the home setting to guide his or her child at the computer were chosen for the study. The children selected reside in Staten Island, New York, and attend local elementary public schools. As in the feasibility study, children who have had exposure to computers in the home setting prior to the commencement of the study were selected. Therefore, for the current study, the participant children had exposure to computers before the age of 6. Adults participating in the study were parents in the household who offered guidance to their children during computer activity time.

In the current study there were five families with dual-parent households and one family with a single-mother as head of household. There were 11 parents in the households of the study families. Only eight parents were available during site visits to guide participating 6-year-old children at home computers. Siblings present during computer time were part of the research environment, but the 6-year-old children and parents who offered guidance to their children interacting with computers were the main participants for the current study. Five of the families had two children and one family had one child.

Participant Selection Criteria

Parents who interact with their children in the home setting were selected to be participants in the current study. This participant selection criterion enabled being able to address research question one: What strategies do these parents utilize to offer their children guidance and access to computers? In households with one parent, selection for participation in the study was decided through the researcher questioning whether or not the adult offered guidance to his or her child at the home computer. When it was a two-parent household, for the family to be selected to participate in the study at least one parent needed to be available to offer guidance to their 6-year-old child at the home computer.

An essential factor for selection of children to participate in the study was that the 6-year-old children had exposure to computers in the home setting prior to age 6. The study explored how parents guide children's emerging computer knowledge, not the initiation of computer interaction. Therefore, the children in the study needed to have previous interactions with computers in the home setting prior to involvement as participants in the current study.

Instruments

Several research instruments were utilized by the researcher for collection of data. During scheduled site visits observation by the researcher, videotaping of activity at the computer, and note-taking were used for data collection. A computer activity sheet was developed and tested to effectively assist in gathering descriptive information about activity at the computer. A long interview questionnaire for parents was developed and tested by the researcher. The parent interviews were conducted to obtain information about parents' perspectives of computers. To accurately record information during site visits and for parent interviews a video camera was used.

For analysis, information was quantified to compare and contrast data collected. A discourse analysis coding sheet was used to transcribe videotaped interviews and observations. The resulting transcriptions enabled tally counts of language categories to emerge. The quantified language categories and parent proximity behaviors were converted to percentages that allowed patterns within and across participants to emerge. The array of instruments that were employed permitted the use of multiple tools to gather information resulting in a qualitative research design and quantitative data analysis to explore the three research questions of the current study.

Note-Taking Using Computer Activity Sheet

By using observation the researcher is able "to draw inferences about someone's meaning and perspective" (Maxwell, 1996, p. 76). During the feasibility study anecdotal notes were taken on blank lined paper. For the current study a computer activity observation sheet was created to record field notes for observations conducted. To enable uniformity of format for site visit field notes, the researcher developed a form that included labels to record the date of the observation, the start as well as end time of the observation, the participant child's name, the participant parent's name, and any other relevant contextual information for each home site visit.

The Computer Activity Observation Sheet (see Appendix A) was field-tested by the researcher. This instrument ensured accurate and consistent recording of the date, adult and child's names, start time, end time, and other related information for each site visit. Observations of activities noted by the researcher, such as actions that occurred beyond the video camera viewing area or nonverbal gestures, were recorded on the activity sheet. Note-taking documentation offered details such as hand position on the computer mouse, facial expressions, or interactions that took place off-camera. Note-taking information supplemented data collected with the video camera.

Use of a Video Camera

To accurately record computer activity during site visits a video camera was utilized during observations. The use of a video camera captures visual information of individual nuances, temporal manifestations, and situational factors that may occur in the research setting (Raingruber, 2003). The video camera recorded verbal and nonverbal actions occurring within view of the camera during visits. The resulting videotapes allowed the researcher to view site visit activities repeatedly and to be able to explore talk and physical movement.

The video camera recorded activity that occurred at the computer, in particular the parent and child's activity during computer time. The video camera recorded verbal and nonverbal activity when a parent was sitting with a child and offering guidance, when a parent offered guidance to a child during independent activity time, or when a child was independently interacting with the hardware and software of a computer.

Parent Computer Perspective Interview

In this study, parent interviews were utilized to attempt to identify parental beliefs about computers and guiding children at the computer. The Parent Computer Perspective Interview (see Appendix B) developed by the researcher contains 20 questions to explore parental views about computers. The six categories created for questions are: (a) general information; (b) household computer information; (c) parent's computer information and use; (d) child's computer information and use; (e) family computer information and use; and (f) parent attitudes about computers. Verbal instructions (see Appendix C) for parents were created to be read to parents before interviews began.

The qualitative tool chosen was long interviews (McCracken, 1988) of parents to allow for the sequential order of questions that would be asked. The use of the long interview format allowed pertinent follow-up questions to be asked that are evoked from adult responses. This offers a structured yet open-ended interview format that provides a consistent basis for data gathering and exploration of limited additional participation interests and concerns.

One of the reasons that parent interviews were conducted was to determine if parents' viewpoints would correspond to observations of parental actions during computer activity time. The videotaped interviews were reviewed and transcribed in preparation for analysis to note parental views, as well as if there was a congruency between perspectives and actions. The resulting data obtained from parent interviews when compared to computer activity observations allowed valid inferences to be drawn that are meaningful for the sample of participants in the current study (Creswell, 2002). Comparison of parent responses to observations of parents interacting with their children permitted triangulation of data being considered.

Another use of parent interviews was to analyze the themes, patterns, and issues that emerged during review of the data. Through examination of adult responses the research question of the significance of computers in their children's lives and common goals for their children's acquisition of computer knowledge were considered. Parent interviews were conducted before site visits began.

The profile of adults for the current study was similar to participants of the feasibility study; they were parents of 6-year-old children, living in Staten Island, New York. The questions developed for the parent interview questionnaire were pilot-tested on adults from the feasibility study. These informants were quite similar to the participants for the current study (Maxwell, 1996).

Developing Parent Interview Questions

Land's (1999) parent/guardian survey instrument was a resource for questions chosen for the verbal interview of parents in the current study. The nine-page, 41-question written survey used a five-response Lickert scale format and an array of questions to elicit information about the times and routines for children's in-home media use. The resulting survey responses were analyzed using descriptive statistics "to determine measures of central tendencies of the sample and the variables" (p. 89).

The current parent interview questions were developed through an iterative field test that provided a grounded basis for the final validity of the interview protocol. The first draft of parent interview questions that was developed for the current study had 50 questions. The survey did not seem to work as intended. Questions seemed too broad and did not elicit necessary information in trying to explore parent views and perspectives. Examples of questions eliminated from the first draft are does he/she (your child) have certain web sites he/she visits often, or describe your child when he/she is using the computer. For the pilot-tested first draft of questions, the parent respondent was succinct and to the point in answering questions. Even with concise responses the interview required approximately one hour to complete. The length of time that would be needed to conduct an interview with 50 questions seemed too long for use with parents.

The second draft of 20 questions reduced the number of questions and refined the concentration of the questions included in the survey. Interview questions were more focused and allowed data related to research questions one and three: Why do you think young children need to learn about how to use computers, or what do you do when you do not understand how to operate the hardware or software of a computer? The revised interview tool was pilot-tested on parents. The resulting parent interviews were able to be conducted in less than one hour and were more focused on gathering responses to the category topic questions.

Validity

According to Creswell (2002), validity in qualitative research may be demonstrated through a variety of approaches. Validity for this qualitative tool, the Parent Computer Perspective Interview questionnaire, is supported by the iterative development cycle used to create and refine the interview protocol. The interview questions would elicit responses from parents that should be able to uncover parental perspectives about how children should be guided at the computer and why knowledge of computers is important.

In qualitative research Maxwell (1996) uses validity to refer to, "the correctness or credibility of a description, conclusion, explanation, or interpretation" (p. 87). Parent interview questions being used in long interviews of parents will allow full, descriptive responses to emerge. The use of prepared questions for each parent who was interviewed allowed an understanding of responses from each parent and across parents, which will allow soundness and accuracy of inferences to emerge.

Reliability

In qualitative research Merriam (1998) perceives reliability as "given the data collected, the results make sense—they are consistent and dependable. The question is not whether findings will be found again but whether the results are consistent with the data collected" (p. 206). A structured and open-ended questionnaire is a reliable tool for an interviewer, as the questions are predetermined and allow participants to respond to a set of questions and add any additional related information the adult may desire (Creswell, 2002; Nardi, 2003). Thus the reliability of the parent interview questionnaire being used for the current study as a qualitative data gathering instrument is supported.

Procedure

The procedure for the current study was to adhere to the following steps: (a) conduct feasibility study; (b) identify the research setting; (c) use feasibility study results of language categories to develop content analysis coding sheet; (d) pilot-test content analysis coding sheet with videotapes from pilot study; (e) pilot-test observation procedure to ensure reliability; (f) develop parent interview questions; (g) conduct pilot-test of interview tool; (h) refine parent interview questions; (i) conduct pilot-test of revised interview tool; (j) obtain appropriate authorization to conduct current research from proper authorities; (k) distribute flyers to recruit participants; (l) talk to parents who contact researcher by telephone or email about participation in study; (m) obtain parent permission for recruited participants to conduct observations; (n) conduct parent interviews; (o) conduct four site visits and compile data during observations of six children and when occurring, parents interacting with children at computers in the home setting; (p) transcribe findings; and (q) analyze data, review findings, and decide recommendations for future studies.

Identification of the Research Setting

The research setting for this study was homes of families residing in Staten Island, New York. These home environments were chosen as the research setting as a replication of home settings used in the feasibility study. The home setting of the participating families was the site where parent interviews and computer activity observations were conducted. The parent interviews were conducted with the participating child not in the area so the child was not able to hear parent responses. The four visits to each home setting to observe activity at the computer were arranged with participating parents to be when the child and parent were available after school, in the evening, or on the weekend.

To be able to conduct the current study, first written permission was sought and obtained from the Institutional Review Board at Fordham University. Next, written permission using an approved Fordham informed consent form was obtained from parents to have their children and themselves participate in the research study. From information obtained in the parent interview the researcher was able to complete the demographics form (see Appendix E).

Participant Recruitment

Information flyers about the study were distributed to elementary public schools in Staten Island to recruit possible participants. Participants were also recruited through acquaintances of the researcher by distributing flyers to families with children age 6. Parents interested in participating contacted the researcher via telephone or email, to notify the researcher of possible interest for participation in the study.

The researcher's initial contact with families was by telephone with an explanation being given for the purpose of the study, as well as the procedure for parent interviews and site visits to the home. To guide selection the researcher asked criteria questions to determine if potential participants had a 6-year-old child who had used a computer before the age of 6, had a computer available for the child's use in the home setting, and if at least one parent was available in the home during the child's time at the computer. During the researcher's first visit, permission forms were signed by the parent who agreed to be interviewed for the study.

Participants

Participants for the current study were six mothers, two fathers, and their six children who were all 6 years of age. As in the feasibility study the children were students currently attending public schools in Staten Island, New York. In this study three of the children were male and three were female. Profile information about parents and additional data on the participants' ethnic background, gender, socioeconomic status, and other data are included in Chapter 4.

Protocol for Observations

Site visit days and times were arranged by the researcher with one parent from each family. Dates were chosen when participating children and one parent would be home and interacting at the computer. The researcher then visited homes at the predetermined times. At the initial site visit meeting the researcher reviewed the protocol of the study with the parent and child participating in the study. The researcher introduced herself to family members present and then reviewed the purpose and procedure of the study. Parents and children were reminded that participation was voluntary and withdrawal could occur at any time without any negative consequences.

Video Camera Protocol

During each observation the researcher set up a video camera on a tripod as unobtrusively as possible in the room where the home computer was located. For four of the families the camera was set up on a tripod to the right of the computer. For two of the families the camera was set up to the left of the computer. The camera was four to six feet away from the child depending on the size of the room. To take notes, the researcher sat at the side of the room in a location behind where the child and computer were located that did not interfere with room traffic flow. Once the camera and researcher were in position, home activity in the area where the computer was located was videotaped. Observations ranged from 30 minutes up to 2 hours depending on how long a child chose to use the computer during the visit.

The video camera protocol that was followed for the feasibility study was employed for the current study. The video camera was placed behind and to the side of the child using the computer. The camera was positioned to view the computer screen and the side of the subject, with a side view of the computer keyboard and mouse. For each session a blank videotape was labeled with the subject, day, and date. During site visits the video camera recorded the activity occurring in the area where the computer was being used. At times the activity was a parent and child at the computer; at other times the participating child was independently interacting with the home computer. Use of a video camera was supplemented with field notes recorded during site visit observations.

Structure of Adult Interviews

Interviews were arranged with one parent from each family for a date prior to the scheduled computer activity site visits. Interview sessions were videotaped and lasted between 20 minutes and 45 minutes. Interviews were scheduled and conducted in each family's home while children participating in the study were not present. Parents responded to 20 open-ended questions about computers in their homes, their personal perspective about computers, their family's use of computers, and their child's use of computers. The interview began with the researcher starting recording with the video camera and then reading the Verbal Instructions for Parent Interview (see Appendix C) to the adult. The interview questions were a guide for the researcher with further discussion and additional questions permitted during interviews. When all 20 questions had been asked and no further discussion occurred the videotaping stopped and the interview was concluded.

DATA ANALYSIS

Collection and analysis of data were from multiple sources during the study: videotaped parent interviews transformed to transcriptions, video camera recordings of computer activity that were transcribed and categorized, and field notes. These sources offered triangulation of information to be able to cross-examine data obtained (Locke, Spirduso, & Silverman, 2000; Maxwell, 1996). The current study utilized both qualitative and quantitative data analysis.

Quantitative analysis was obtained from discourse between a parent and child at the computer, as well as language categories parents used to guide their children at the computer. Descriptive information was obtained from review of the researcher's field notes, videotapes, and transcriptions from observations as well as parent interviews. Information gained was used to corroborate or refute results obtained from observation sheets, content analysis coding sheets, and parental interviews. Review of both quantitative and qualitative data enabled conclusions to be drawn about interactions that transpired when adults guided children at the computer.

The use of triangulation of information is a means to "strengthen a study by combining methods or data" (Patton, 2002, p. 247). Denzin's (1978) study considered the use of an array of data sources as a type of triangulation, which is identified as data triangulation. The information collected from the interviews, observations, and videotapes enabled data triangulation.

Mele Robinson Content Analysis Coding Sheet

Videotaped data was transcribed into running transcripts of both verbal and nonverbal activity at the computer, in order to analyze talk and activity that occurred. The transcriptions were placed in table format to code according to the elements of the Mele Robinson Content Analysis Coding Sheet (see Appendix D). The discourse elements coded were the language utilized by both parent and child at the computer as well as the nonverbal actions that occurred at the computer. Themes and patterns were identified within the transcripts as text fields to be grouped and sorted by emerging variables.

One aspect of the recorded data that was examined is the quantity of each language category used by parents when guiding children during time at the computer. The number of times directive language, procedural language, validating language, inquiry language, or conversational language were used was considered. The total usage in each language category for each parent and between parents was examined to consider the recurrent types of language categories parents use when guiding children at the computer.

Discourse that occurred at the computer as an adult interacted and guided a young child was coded using discourse coding categories developed. The coding tool was built on concepts from talk at the computer between individuals and Cazden's unmarked pattern of traditional language during school lessons (2001, p. 31). When available, physical context cues such as gestures, proximity, and movement of hands or direction of eyes were also noted on the coding sheet.

The purpose of using this instrument to code discourse was to be able to categorize language used by adults talking to children during time at the computer. Discourse occurring between adults and children was categorized using the Mele Robinson Content Analysis Coding Sheet (see Appendix D) sheet for discourse categories of initiation, response, discussion, and feedback at the computer. Initiation is who begins discussion during time at the computer. Discussion is talk occurring at the computer. Response is answering what was asked (by a person) at the computer. Follow-up discussion is additional conversations that build on an initial response given by an individual.

The coding sheet was pilot-tested by the researcher using videotapes from the feasibility study. This instrument was tested using different researchers and the resulting coding offered consistent results, which confirmed the tool's reliability. The researcher transcribed a section of the site visit videotape for parent language and parent-child discourse at the computer. A graduate psychology student also coded the same videotaped section. The two raters each completed the same coding sheet with very similar results obtained. Interrater reliability for the raters' review of the coding sheet was 0.85. The use of the coding sheet allowed parent-child discourse, parent language, and nonverbal actions to be categorized.

Parent Interview Videotape Review

The parent interviews were videotaped, transcribed, and analyzed. The purpose of the interview tool was to gain information about the type of computer equipment in participants' homes, how learning to use computers has occurred for parents as well as their children, how computers are used by children and their parents, parental views of the importance of computers in children's lives, and how parents guide children at the computer. Based on Land's (1999) approach to data analysis, the resulting data were compared among participants with tabulations and cross-tabulations which allowed an understanding of similarities and differences among parents, children, or families for:

- type of computer equipment in homes
- parent workplace computer use
- place of initial use of computers by parents
- how learning to use computers occurred for parents
- strategies used when parents need guidance at the computer

Patterns and themes that emerged from parent responses allowed relationships among variables to be considered. This data analysis responded to research question three: What do these parents consider the significance of computers in their children's lives and what are common goals for their children's acquisition of computer knowledge? Data analysis for the parent interview responses began immediately after finishing the first interview and analysis of data continued throughout the research process. Review of interview videotapes, computer activity observation sheets, and transcriptions offered triangulation of information and reduced the risk of conclusions being due to chance associations.

The use of both note-taking and videotaping increased the quality of the observations which augmented the reliability of the data. The observations conducted, as well as the evidence collected, have internal consistency because the same room was used by participants for each home visit, the same computer was used, and the same adults and children were observed interacting at home computers. The resulting information produced evidence based on equivalent forms. Careful criteria were developed for procedures and protocols which increased reliability and objectivity of this study.

FEASIBILITY STUDY

The feasibility study was conducted (a) to determine the suitability of the instruments and procedures chosen for the current study, (b) to explore the ways parents guide young children when interacting at a home computer, (c) to explore the strategies that young children utilize when independently interacting with computers, and (d) to decide the appropriateness of using videotaped observations to try to understand how parents and young children interact at the computer. To be able to conduct the feasibility study, written permission was sought and obtained from the Institutional Review Board at Fordham University.

Feasibility Study Participants

Families with a computer that was available to children in their home settings were selected for participation in the pilot study. The two 6-year-old children and their parents lived in Staten Island, New York. The children were both first grade students attending New York City Department of Education public elementary schools in Staten Island, New York. Neither student was eligible for free school lunches.

The male participant, Michael, and the female participant, Emily, were both White American. In the school setting the male child had access to computers in the classroom. The female child did not have computers in her classroom but was enrolled in an after-school computer class at her elementary school. The children had been interacting with a computer in the home setting since at least the age of 3. The parents who interacted with their children while computer activity occurred in the home setting were Michael's mother, and Emily's mother or father. During site visits at least one parent was in the home setting while the 6-year-old child interacted with a home computer.

Feasibility Study Setting

The setting for the feasibility study was in the home of each family participating in the research study. The participants lived in private homes located in Westerleigh, a community in Staten Island, New York. The setting for computer activity was on the first floor of each home for the two families participating in the case study. There were two 6-year-old children in the study, one male (Michael) and one female (Emily). Michael's computer was located on the main table of the dining room area. Emily's computer was located in the first room of the household by the entrance foyer. For each family the computer was located in a high-traffic area of the home where a parent was easily able to be aware of the child's computer activity. Each child used the same home computer during all site visits. The computer that was used belonged to the family and not to the individual child.

Feasibility Study Procedure

The focus of the feasibility study was the observation of young children using a computer in the home setting. Written permission was sought after and obtained from the Institutional Review Board at Fordham University. Families with 6-year-old children were recruited by the researcher from personal social contacts. This selection process was purposeful since families with computers in their homes needed to be chosen for the study. Potential families were contacted and the research process was explained to parents. The researcher explained the purpose of the study and the process of site visits with activity at the computer to be videotaped. Written permission was obtained from parents for each child chosen and for parents involved.

Dates and times were arranged for the researcher's first site visit to observe and videotape computer activity in the home setting. As site visits continued, subsequent dates and times were decided upon. In total, each home was visited four times for observations of activity at the computer. Recorded videotapes as well as anecdotal notes were reviewed for recurring patterns, strategies, and approaches used by the children and their parents during time at the computer. From the information obtained, data were analyzed for resulting perceptions and hypotheses.

Protocol for Feasibility Study Observations

At the initial meeting with families, the researcher reviewed the purpose and procedure that would be followed during site visits. Parents and children were told that the researcher would be coming to visit to observe how children and parents interact with computers. The researcher explained to the families that a video camera would be used and notes would be written to document what happened at the computer. Parents and children were reminded that participation was voluntary and withdrawal could have occurred at any time without any negative consequences.

Video Camera and Note-Taking During Observations

For the feasibility study, times were selected when participating children and one parent were at home. The researcher visited homes at the predetermined times and during each visit followed the same procedure for setting up equipment as well as utilizing the note-taking protocols. Each videotape was labeled with the subject's name and date. At the beginning of each observation, the researcher set up the video camera on a tripod as unobtrusively as possible in the room where the home computer was located. The video camera was placed slightly behind and to the side of the child at the computer. The camera was situated so the activity of a subject or subjects, the computer screen, and the computer keyboard could be viewed by the camera during videotaping. The researcher sat at the perimeter of the room at a location that did not interfere with room traffic flow. Once the camera and researcher were in position, home activity in the area where the computer was located was videotaped.

The researcher's anecdotal note-taking supplemented the use of the video camera during site visits. Note-taking was used to record activity observed that occurred beyond the camera viewing area such as body language, hand movements, facial expressions, and interactions in adjacent room areas. Observations varied between 60 minutes and 2 hours depending on whether a child chose to use the computer during the first 60 minutes of the site visit.

Feasibility Study Results

The data obtained through utilization of video camera recordings as well as note-taking offered triangulation through the gathering of information from a variety of sources (Maxwell, 1996). The information derived from review of the videotapes and notes taken during observations allowed information to be gained about adults interacting with young children at the computer along with children's independent computer activity time. Language categories emerged for language used by adults during interaction with children at the computer. Activity categories for young children engaged in independent interaction with a home computer surfaced. For the hypotheses-generating feasibility study, information was obtained from common experiences, actions, strategies, and activities which occurred at the home computer for each child or between parents and their children. During review of videotape recordings and note-taking data, an item was considered significant if the researcher noted that the action or language category occurred repeatedly, at least five or more times, in both children or for both parents and children.

Feasibility Study Parents Offering Access to Computers

Both families in the feasibility study had more than one computer in the home. The children used a desktop computer located in the general shared family area of the household. These children began using computers with parental guidance at about the age of 3. The access to home computers allowed these children to use a computer before beginning elementary school. Now at age 6, these children use computers at school. Access to the computer in the home setting provided these children with computer experience before entering a formal school setting.

Feasibility Study Parental Guidance at the Computer

The adults observed in the feasibility study were all parents of the children participating in the study. During each site visit at least one parent present would offer assistance to the child at the computer sometime during the visit. The two approaches used by these parents when offering their children guidance were having a parent in close physical proximity to the computer or a parent sitting with a child and working together at the computer.

During different site visits the researcher observed as a parent was in the general area near the computer that a child was using. For example, 6-year-old Michael was interacting with the computer at the dining room table and his mother was in the kitchen, an adjacent room with an open doorway. She would visually check on her son frequently while he interacted with the home computer. If her son had a question or this parent noticed her child could not successfully complete a computer task, she would ask questions such as, "Are you okay?" or "Do you know how that game works?" By being in close proximity parents were available to offer guidance.

There were times during site visits that the researcher observed as a parent and child worked together to resolve computer issues. Through cooperative problem solving, a parent and child would try to decide where to go next while playing computer software games or how to get the computer hardware to perform what the pair was trying to accomplish. At times the child took the lead and at other times the adult assumed the lead in these problem-solving endeavors. As Facer et al. (2003) found, learning in the home setting often involves "a more genuinely collaborative enterprise in which both parent and child is 'co-constructing' knowledge" (p. 192). A collaborative approach to learning at the computer was observed in both home settings. The adults in the feasibility study seemed comfortable with their children offering suggestions and at times solving computer challenges.

Feasibility Study Identification of Language Categories

The categories of language used by parents that emerged in the feasibility study were directive language, procedural language, validating language, and inquiry language. Directive language was language used to give directions for what needed to be implemented when a child was using computer hardware or software without an explanation of why the procedure was needed. Examples of such language were, "Go there" as a parent pointed to the computer screen or "Double click on the door" when a parent wanted a child to access an entry point during game play.

Procedural language was used to explain a series of steps needed to accomplish certain software program results or hardware responses from a computer. An adult would tell a child what to do and explain the reason for the action that needed to be taken. When the female subject's father was going to load a software program onto the computer he explained the procedure to his daughter. He told her, "You hold the CD-ROM like this" (he demonstrated and then handed the CD-ROM to the child) "and you put it in the tray here because that's how you begin to load the program on the computer."

Validating language was the use of language that offered encouragement through positive verbal reinforcement for an individual's attempt with an activity. The adults in the feasibility study used validating language often and the positive verbal reinforcement seemed to encourage their children to continue to interact with the home computer. Parental responses such as "That's great" or "Wow, look at what you made!" received smiles, laughs, and continued computer interaction from the children in the feasibility study.

Inquiry language was used by parents to clarify or question a child's action at the computer. Asking questions allowed the adults to check for their children's understanding of what was being done at the computer or with the computer. Then the parents would know what guidance at the computer was needed. For example, 6-year-old Emily's mother Eileen asked, "Do you know how to turn the computer on?" Emily knew the procedure to follow, but if she did not Eileen would have told her the sequence to use when booting up the computer. The language categories used by parents that emerged in the feasibility study of directive language, procedural language, validating language, and inquiry language allowed the children to continue to successfully engage with the home computer.

After completion of the feasibility study and upon reflection of language used at the computer, the researcher added the language category of conversational language. Conversational language is talk that occurred at the computer which focused on activity occurring with the computer or talk about activities not related to computer activity. This additional language category was not used for the feasibility study but was incorporated into the language categories of the current study.

Feasibility Study Children's Independent Activity Categories

During the feasibility study when interacting with computer hardware or software, the children observed attempted a variety of approaches to be able to sustain computer activity interaction. The researcher observed that as the study children, Emily and Michael, interacted with a home computer there were times the children could successfully interact with a computer's hardware or software by following procedural methods the child knew from previous computer interactions. The researcher observed as the male participant, Michael, manipulated the menu of the art program he played often. He would go to the menu to decide which program activity he wanted to play. He knew the procedure to adhere to in order to successfully engage with the drawing software program.

The data collected via videotape and from note-taking demonstrated that at times the children would try experimentation at the computer with new and purposeful computer tactics, which built on previous computer knowledge. For example, female participant Emily understood how to shut the computer off by following the reverse of what she had done to turn the computer on. The researcher observed as she verbally guided herself by stating the sequential steps aloud as she completed the process. This purposeful experimentation was able to be duplicated at other times when the child turned the computer off.

When interacting with a home computer, at times the children would successfully complete a hardware or software challenge but could not duplicate the experimentation. This non-duplicative action of trial and error seemed to occur by chance and the child could not explain or replicate the action. For example, the researcher observed as 6-year-old Emily clicked the mouse repeatedly on different locations of the computer screen. When the software program reacted and the computer screen changed the child seemed pleased as she smiled at the screen. In an effort to understand the child's action, the researcher asked Emily how she completed the maneuver and she responded, "I don't know."

Facer et al. (2003) noted this same phenomenon during observations: there seemed to be some experimentation that occurred which could *not* be duplicated by the study children and some experimentation which could be duplicated by the children during independent activity time. Further study of this particular aspect of children's independent activity at the computer would be needed to clarify when and how actions at the computer could be considered duplicative or non-duplicative. The importance of understanding the difference between these two subcategories of independent activity is that at first a child's actions seem to occur by chance and then as more knowledge is gained the child's actions appear to be more purposeful.

The researcher observed as a child attempted exploration of computer hardware or software. After attaining initial success through experimentation with understanding how to interact with a computer, a child independently explored the software program or manipulation of the computer hardware to gain additional information. The children were observed during the action of traveling in or through an unfamiliar area of computer interaction in order to understand more about a certain aspect of the computer's hardware or software. For example, Michael was observed trying to interact with a new aspect of his favorite drawing software program and stated aloud, "Let's see what this does." After using the new program element the child laughed and tried the task over again. Building on initial experimentation with the home computer with exploration of new strategies allowed expansion of the children's knowledge of how to use the computer.

The feasibility study approaches that appeared to be successful and were able to sustain independent computer interaction for the children observed were following a familiar procedural approach, the use of experimentation (duplicative and non-duplicative), and attempting exploration of how to interact with the home computer. The children's independent activity categories were not part of the current study. The current study focused primarily on parents guiding children at the computer.

Feasibility Study Participant Reaction to Researcher

In the feasibility study the presence of the researcher did not appear to impede computer activity that occurred in the home setting. If the study children did want to interact with the computer, the children did so without talking to or seeking approval from the researcher. The parents seemed clear that the researcher was in the home to be an observer. After greeting parents and children upon entering the home and setting up equipment, the researcher tried to refrain from engaging in conversations with family members during site visit observations. Using the same approach again in the current study allowed the results obtained to offer reliable data for the research topic being explored.

Feasibility Study Discussion

The results of the feasibility study showed the approaches used by parents to guide their children and the strategies employed by children independently interacting with computers in the home setting. When parents assisted children at the computer, the adults did so at times by being in the general area where the computer was located and observing that the child needed assistance. At other times parents sat with children during computer activity time to offer guidance. When working together at the computer, collaborative problem solving was at times an approach chosen for solving computer quandaries.

The language categories utilized by adults were directive language, procedural language, validating language, and inquiry language. Validating language that offered encouragement for children during time at the computer was employed by all parents regardless of parent computer proficiency levels. In some circumstances the validating language used and not the parent's computer knowledge was the factor that seemed to sustain computer time. Therefore, parents' physical proximity and language used were factors that seemed to encourage and offer guidance for young children interacting with a home computer.

When working independently at the computer the 6-year-old children used procedural knowledge, experimentation, or exploration to sustain interaction with the computer hardware or software. These strategies enabled the children to continue to successfully interact with the home computer's hardware or software. The results of the feasibility study offer information, which assisted in forming the current research.

Recommendations Resulting from Feasibility Study

From the findings of the feasibility study, the following recommendations for the current study were able to be made:

1. Review of videotapes from site visit observations was a strategy used to analyze feasibility study video camera recordings. The current study seeks to consider both qualitative analysis and quantitative data results, by making use of the Mele Robinson Content Analysis Coding Sheet (see Appendix D) categorizations. The transcribed results of discourse occurring at the computer offered tallies for adult language categories occurring and talk between parent and child at the computer.

2. Activities occurring at the computer for children and parents were explored in the feasibility study. The current study focused more on parents guiding children at the computer. By focusing on parental behaviors in relation to how young children's computer knowledge develops, the current study was able to offer an in-depth exploration of the dynamics occurring at the computer between adults and children.

3. In the feasibility study, note-taking and video camera recording were used to obtain an understanding of how parents offered guidance and access for children at the computer. In the current study, note-taking and video camera recording continued to be used. Parent interviews were added to the research instruments to delve further into the adult's perspectives and beliefs about computers. The data obtained from the parent interviews assisted with triangulation of information.

The feasibility study provided essential information, which guided the structure of the current study. The changes incorporated from lessons learned in the feasibility study were crucial in being able to refine and pilot-test instruments, as well as develop the current qualitative/quantitative research design. Focusing on parents guiding young children at computers in the home setting is the central focus of the current study.

4 Research Findings

Approaches offered by parents guiding young children interacting with computers in the home setting are examined in this study. This chapter describes data findings for the participant parents and their 6-year-old children and delves into both qualitative and quantitative study results. Data in the form of strategies, practices, patterns, similarities, and differences within and among parents guiding their children at home computers were collected, analyzed, and interpreted. The findings of the study are utilized to respond to the research questions presented in the study:

1. What strategies do these parents utilize to offer their children guidance and access to computers?
2. What language categories and patterns do these parents utilize to guide their young children interacting with computers?
3. What do these parents consider the significance of computers in their children's lives and what are common goals for their children's acquisition of computer knowledge?

METHODOLOGY UTILIZED FOR THE ANALYSIS OF DATA

This case study is about parents guiding children at the computer. The data collected and analyzed for this study focused on understanding: (a) the strategies used by parents to guide and offer computer access to their children, (b) the discourse and language categories used by these parents to guide their children interacting with computers, and (c) what the parents in this study consider the significance of computers in their children's lives and common goals for their children's acquisition of computer knowledge. Data were collected in several ways for the study: parent interviews, researcher observations and note-taking, as well as videotaping of activity at the computer during home visits.

The researcher videotaped six parent interviews and the four site visits to each of the six families' homes where computer activity occurred. Each site visit was approximately 1–2 hours in length. Transcriptions were developed from videotaped parent interviews and the four site visits with each family. The resulting information provided descriptive qualitative data that assisted in responding to research questions one and three.

To respond to research question two, the resulting transcriptions were analyzed using the Mele Robinson Content Analysis Coding Sheet (see Appendix D). Detailed analysis of participant parents' adult language, as well as categorization of talk, revealed the type of language and talk occurring at the computer between participant parents and their 6-year-old children. The data collected includes six parent interviews and four site visits for each of the six participant families. Therefore there was data collected from 24 site visits. These data offer a wealth of information to consider how parents guide their young children during home computer activity time.

PARTICIPANTS

Demographics and computer information about study participant family members is presented in summary form in the Family Information charts of Table 4.1. This chart presents participant children's pseudonyms with detailed information about personal and educational information for the study children and their parents. Information about the type of computer utilized and its location in the home is included. As in the feasibility study the 6-year-old children are students currently attending public schools in Staten Island, New York. None of the children are eligible for the free lunch program at their schools.

The ethnicity of all parents was White non-Hispanic and the children were predominantly White non-Hispanic. Mothers were age 35 and older with fathers being 39 years of age and older. Parents for the six families have attained a range of educational experiences including high school diplomas, radiology technician certification, bachelor degrees, and Masters in Education degrees. There was one parent enrolled in a four-year early childhood education degree program and another in a medical assistant certification program.

The population of Staten Island is comprised of 70% White non-Hispanics, 13% Hispanics, and 10% Black or African Americans (NCES, 2001). The ethnicity of family members in the current study was 91% White non-Hispanic and 9% Asian.

Educational information for Staten Islanders indicates that 84% of individuals age 25 or older are high school graduates with 23% attaining a bachelors degree or higher. For the six families, 100% of adults have high school diplomas and 45% have a bachelors degree or higher. The population sample of the study is not representative of the general Staten Island population for ethnicity or educational attainment of adults.

Table 4.1 Family Information: Demographics and Computers

Child's name	Home	Computer(s) and locations	Child's main use	Mother's main use	Father's main use
Patrick Jr.	Own, single-family, Attached 2 floors	(1) PC in basement Family Room	Software programs & children's web sites	Emails	Emails
Victoria	Own, single-family, Detached 2 floors	(1) PC in Dining Room & (1) PC in brother's room	Software programs	Own school work, weather, events, calendar, paying bills	—
Samantha	Own, single-family, Detached 2 floors	(1) PC in Dining Room & (1) PC in basement Family Room	Software programs	Internet, local events and information, Word	Internet
Ashley	Own, single-family, Detached, 1 floor	(1) PC in parent's bedroom	Software programs	Internet, college work	Internet, Word
Eric	Own, single-family, Detached, 2 floors	(1) PC in Dining Room	Software programs & children's web sites	Information, Emails	Word
Kyle	Own, single-family, Detached, 2 floors	(1)PC in Den	Children's web sites & Godzilla web site	Information, Internet shopping	Internet

PC = personal computer
Word = Microsoft Word program

The current study included six families with a total of six mothers, two fathers, and six children 6 years of age involved with computer activity time. The participant children assigned pseudonyms for themselves and each study participant family member. The resulting name choices and participant family members are presented in Table 4.2. The pseudonyms include the names of family members interacting at the home computer during the researcher's site visits, including the 6-year-old participant children, siblings, and parents who assisted children during time at the computer.

RESEARCH QUESTION ONE

This qualitative/quantitative study examined parents and children's interactions while children were utilizing a home computer. The first research question is: What strategies do these parents utilize to offer their children guidance and access to computers? Through the use of videotaped parental interviews, the researcher collected data regarding this question. Data were also collected via researcher field notes, and videotaped home visits, which documented parent-child computer interactions. Collected videotaped data were transcribed and analyzed, resulting in the creation of multiple tables and figures. The research results are an interpretation by the researcher of documented strategies utilized by these particular parents to guide and offer access to home computers for their children. Common characteristics across parents for computer guidance with regard to proximity of parents

Table 4.2   Family Member Pseudonyms

Family	6-Year-Old Child's Name	Other Family Members
1	Patrick Jr.	Mother-Christina
		Father-Patrick Sr.
2	Victoria	Mother-Elizabeth
		Brother-Joe
3	Samantha	Mother-Jean
		Sister-Olivia
4	Ashley	Mother-Gina
		Brother-Christopher
5	Eric	Mother-Aileen
		Sister-Jaime
6	Kyle	Mother-Barbara
		Father-Michael
		Brother-Joseph

to their children, consistency of parents offering assistance to their children, as well as issues of parents offering their children computer access will be discussed in this section.

Adults Guiding Children with Computers

When responding to the ways adults are able to guide children developing an understanding of how to use computers, parents were clear and enthusiastic about the strategies they thought should be used. Patrick Sr. the father of Family 1 said, "Just spending time with them (children) as opposed to sitting there on the boob tube, sitting there watching TV . . . make it learning time, make it fun, buy some of the learning games . . . and you (parents) can sit down then with them (children) and you can see a big difference on how they can concentrate and focus on everything." Gina, the mother of Family 4, considers development occurring by "Learning themselves. They have to learn themselves first . . . if you (parent) know how to use the computer, and you sit with your child, and you sit *on* the computer with your child, that's how they're going to learn, that's the only way. Not sitting here talking to them about it, actually showing them how to do it." Parents conveyed specific possibilities of how adults might guide children learning to use computers.

When analyzing and interpreting data regarding the first research question, two common themes emerged relating to how parents in this study guided their children at the home computer. One theme that emerged was the congruency between what parents reported during parent interviews in regard to their perspectives of how children develop an understanding of how to use computers and what parents actually did or said during the observation periods. Another theme that emerged included parents being in close proximity when telling or showing their child how to interact with a computer's hardware or software. Within this theme emerged parental consistency of offering guidance to their children when assistance was needed. The following section explains these patterns that were observed by the researcher in parents' responses and actions.

Congruency of Parent Perspectives to Parent Actions

Parent interview responses offered parents' viewpoints about children developing an understanding of how to use computers. The researcher's field notes, videotapes, and transcriptions of parent actions during computer activity offered information about how parents actually guided their children at the computer. One of the goals of data analysis was to gauge the congruency of parental perspectives offered during parent interviews and what parents did to guide their children at the computer. The results allowed valid meaningful inferences to be drawn for the sample of participants in this study.

The parent interview question in particular that explored parents' perspectives about activity at the computer was: What ways can adults guide children developing an understanding of how to use computers? A summary is given in Table 4.3 of parent responses, along with parent actions, and if there is congruency between parent's perspective and parent's actions. For example, for Family 4 a summary of the parent's response to Question 19 was "Sit on the computer with your child . . . actually showing them what to do." During the first site visit the researcher observed that for Family 4 the child was using an educational web site for the first time. The mother of Family 4, Gina, sat next to her child, Ashley, and explained what to do to use an unfamiliar web site. On subsequent site visits the child was not using any new software or web sites and was mainly able to use the computer independently. She would call her mother when she needed assistance with a computer problem such as the mouse not operating properly because of a tangled wire. When Ashley called her mother, assistance would be offered; whether the guidance was showing her daughter what to do to use a new web site or how to resolve the problem of computer equipment not functioning properly.

Therefore, there was a congruency between the parent perspective of how children learn to use computers and how this parent guided her child during computer activity time. The observation results by the researcher allowed valid meaningful inferences to be drawn for the sample of participants in this study. For each parent in the current study, the resulting review of data verified congruency between parental perspectives about how children learn to use computers and parent actions at the computer when guiding their children. Parent actions confirmed congruency with parent perspectives.

Proximity

When parents in the study were guiding their children during computer activity, being in close proximity was a commonly used approach that seemed to allow parents to enable their child to continue sustained interaction with the computer. The distance a parent stood in relation to their child at the computer gauged the proximity of parent to child. For the purpose of this study, *close proximity* is considered a parent being 1–5 feet from their child. *General close proximity* was when a parent was 1–7 feet from their child and the home computer. *Not-in-close proximity,* for the purpose of this study, is used to describe when a parent was 8 feet or more from their child and the computer.

Proximity of parents to their children for the majority of site visit time is presented for each family in Table 4.4. For three of the families, parental proximity was usually 1–7 feet from their child during the majority of computer activity time. For the other three families, parents were 8 feet or more from their child, which is not-in-close proximity during the majority of site

Table 4.3   Parent Congruency of Perspective to Action

Family	Parent Response to Question 19	Parent Actions	Congruency
1	Just being involved. You have to be involved with your children. In everything. (Children) have to know when playtime is and when (it) is fun time.	Parents were clearly involved with child's learning experience.	Yes
2	Let them (children) explore on it (computers).	Parent allowed child to independently interact with computer while checking on child's activity.	Yes
3	Letting them (children) know there is a difference between the educational software and junk (poor quality games).	Parent guided child in software selection and educational activities were often included in computer activities chosen.	Yes
4	Sit on the computer with your child . . . actually showing them what to do.	For first visit parent guided child when using new web site. For other visits child independently used computer, calling mother for assistance when needed.	Yes
5	It's a learning process for both of us.	Child usually independently used computer but called mother when there was a problem. At times cooperatively tried to solve computer challenges together.	Yes
6	Show them what to do.	Child independently used computer. Called parent when assistance was needed and adult role modeled what to do to correct problem.	Yes

Table 4.4 Overall Proximity of Parents in Feet during Majority of Site Visit Time

Family	General Proximity	Proximity When Assisting Child
1	1–5	1–5
2	1–5	1–5
3	1–7	1–5
4	10+	1–5
5	8+	1–5
6	15+	1–5

visit activity. At times, parents not-in-close proximity might stop in the room where their child was interacting with the home computer and check on their child's computer activity. For the majority of visits the not-in-close proximity parents were either in a different room or on another floor of the home while their child interacted with the home computer.

For three of the children, Eric, Kyle, and Ashley, in the not-in-close proximity group, their parents would be sure the children were set to use the computer and would then go to another area of the home. These three parents would be sure the computer was on, was running properly, and not causing the children any difficulties. Then each parent would mention to their child to call if any assistance was needed. As Ashley's mother said during her parent interview, "Scream my name, Ma! That always works." For most of the site visits this group of parents was not-in-close proximity to their children during the children's time at the computer.

Routinely, when there were computer difficulties due to a technical hardware glitch or software challenge that interfered with sustained interaction with the computer, the children in the not-in-close proximity group would call for a parent's assistance. At that time the not-in-close proximity parents often asked a clarifying question about what was happening with the computer and would then move within closer proximity of 1–5 feet to offer assistance. For parents who were in close proximity when their children encountered a problem, the difficulty could be verified by the adult's observations of the child's actions, discussion, or questions.

For the not-in-close proximity group of parents, proximity to their children and the home computer ranged from being next to their children to being on another floor of the house. This range did not influence the parent's response or reaction if their children needed assistance with the computer. Every time a child requested assistance at the computer, these parents might ask a clarifying question and would then move closer to their child to try to help solve the difficulty. Whether a parent was in another room or another floor of the home before the child asked for assistance, as soon as the child called, "Mom" or "Dad" these parents would physically come closer to their child and offer assistance. Therefore, a common strategy for parents not-in-close proximity was to respond verbally when called to assist and to move in close proximity when offering assistance.

A parent was either already in close proximity to the child and computer or would move within close proximity to the child interacting with the computer when assistance was needed. From the researcher's site observations and videotape review, one consistent strategy that every parent used when offering their children computer guidance was to be in close proximity when guiding their children at the computer. Proximity of parents to their children while the children interacted with a home computer permitted children to have continuous interaction with the computer.

Consistency

During the 24 site visits any time children asked for computer assistance help was offered. Some parents would first ask the child a clarifying question to understand what the problem with the computer was. Then the parent would move closer to where the child and computer were and would try to be of assistance. At times, a study parent could not resolve the problem of a computer not running a CD-ROM software program properly or could not be of assistance with their child's attempts to access a desired web site; still, every child's request was given a parent's attention and parents consistently attempted to solve computer dilemmas that arose.

For these parents one strategy for guiding their children at the computer included consistently being responsive to the children's need for assistance. The 6-year-old children could depend on the reliability of their parent's being responsive when assistance was needed at the computer for challenges encountered. A common strategy utilized by all study parents was that when their child requested assistance a parent would respond.

Common Characteristics of Computer Access Across Parents

Parents may provide their young children with many experiential opportunities to interact with the world around them. Parents may read to their children, take their children to the library, or show their children how to peddle a tricycle. Parents offering their children access to a variety of experiences and adventures allow a child to learn, grow, and explore. This is the case with parents providing access to computers for their young children. These parents began to offer their children access to computers at the young age of 2 or 3 years. Parents in the current study offered their children access to computers in the home setting and in locations such as school, the library, or an after-school program. In this section common ways that participant parents offered their children access to computers will be presented.

Access to Computers

The videotaped and transcribed parent interviews enabled the researcher to analyze, interpret, and describe participant parents' perspectives for the question of providing their children with access to computers. In response to Question 18 for the topic of parents offering their children access to computers, parent interview responses describe the range of possibilities for exposure they offered to their 6-year-old children for computers. The parents interviewed perceive the significance of computers and computer use extending beyond the home setting. The range of locations for exposure to computers outside the home includes the library, school, after-school classes, a friend's house, or a relative's home. The response of Jean, the mother of Family 3, was "By buying one (computer) if you can. Or you can take them to the library. In school." Jean also discussed with the researcher how her daughter has access to computers in a variety of settings and at various times. Her child, Samantha, uses a computer at her husband's gym, after class at the martial arts school her daughter attends, and at the library by their vacation home. Aileen, the mother in Family 5, described her son's exposure to computers at home and also school: "At school and here (home). Fridays they (children in Eric's class) have computer . . . he goes to after-school center on Friday also, and he takes computer, and that was ever since the beginning of kindergarten."

Access Locations for Children to Interact with Computers

Through parent responses during parent interviews, data was obtained to understand the first research question: What strategies do these parents utilize to offer their children guidance and access to computers? Question 18 of the Parent Computer Perspective Interview is: How do you think adults can provide children with access to computers? Parent responses to this interview question and their discussion of computer access during the parent interviews permitted the issue of parents offering their children access to computers to be explored.

As noted in Table 4.5, all parents in the current study offered their children opportunities to have access to computers in locations outside the home setting. These participating parents considered computer use to be of enough importance that all parents had locations besides home and school where their children had an opportunity to interact with computers. During parent interview discussions most of the parents mentioned that their children did use computers at their friends' homes. This computer use was considered a social situation and these parents did not refer to this access point when discussing where their children used computers.

The library was the location that four of the families chose as an option for access to computers outside the home setting. For example, for one child who had two computers in the home setting, her mother stated that "my

Table 4.5   Locations Parents Offer their Children Access to Computers

Family	Location
1	Library, school
2	Library, school
3	Library, school, after martial arts class
4	Library, school, grandparent's home
5	School, after-school computer class
6	School, after-school computer class

daughter especially loves to go on the computer at the library . . . there's usually a line . . . you put your name on the list and you wait." Although the library was visited to select books, this parent was willing to wait and allow her child to use the one computer available for children in the local library. For Families 5 and 6 their sons were enrolled in a computer class in the school's after-school program. One strategy utilized by all study parents was to offer their children access to computers when possible as part of the child's routine for activities. For all parents in the current study access to computers was offered to their children in the home setting, at school, and also at one additional location.

Computer Ownership and Initial Access to Computers

One of the criteria for participation in the current study was that families had to have a computer in the home. These parents owned a home computer and allowed their children access to a computer in the home setting. Computer ownership was a primary strategy utilized by all participant parents in offering their children access to computers.

Four of the families had one computer in the home and two families had two computers. During interviews parents discussed having two computers. The parent of Family 3 described the second computer as an older hand-me-down unit that had been used in the parent's workplace (and was no longer needed). For Family 2, the older home computer was a unit that was still kept in working order when a newer computer was purchased. For both of these families, the older computer was designated for the children in the family. In the Family 2 household, there were two computers with one specifically designated for the children. The 6-year-old child Victoria had access to both home computers. The computer for the children was located in an older sibling's room and the newer computer was in a place more centrally located in the home. All parents offered their children computer access in the home setting but parents did not state that the home computer was purchased specifically for their children.

For five of the six children, exposure to computers first occurred in the home setting (see Table 4.6). For Eric exposure to computers first occurred in

Table 4.6 Child's Age and Location of Initial Computer Exposure

Child's Name	Age of Introduction	Location
Patrick Jr.	2	Home
Victoria	3	Home
Samantha	2	Home
Ashley	2	Home
Eric	3	Preschool
Kyle	3	Home

the school setting. When he was 3 years old, Eric first interacted with computers at the nursery school he was attending. Soon after, his parents purchased a computer for their home. For three of the children, a home computer had been available since the age of 2. For the other three children a computer had been in the home setting since age 3 (see Table 4.6). Availability of a home computer for their children from the age of 2 or 3 occurred for the families involved in this study. Parents were not specifically asked if the purchase of a home computer was to offer their child access to computers. As a result, the availability of a home computer for participant children from the age of 2 or 3 could not be determined as coincidence or purposeful.

When examining ways participant parents offered their children access to computers, there were several common approaches exhibited in all homes where this study was conducted. One common approach was that access to computers in the home setting was initiated by study parents when their children were at the young age of 2 or 3. Another common theme uncovered was that all the parents in the study offered home computer access to every child in their respective families.

Computer Access Outside of the Home Setting

Parents of young children have a deciding influence for where a child is able to have access to computers. In addition to offering computer access in the home setting, parents may enable their child's access to computers in settings outside of the home. Children may have access to computers at school, at libraries, or a friend's or relative's house. Since the age of the children in the study is 6 years old, the children needed parent permission or parent assistance to be taken to an after-school computer class, the library, or to a friend's or relative's house.

A strategy utilized by five out of the six parents who participated in this study was to offer computer access to their children in settings outside the home. Two of the participant parents have their sons enrolled in a Friday after-school computer class at their community public school. The two boys in the computer class attend the same public school, which offers the program for a small fee. Two other parents present their children with opportunities to make use of computers at public libraries. During parent interviews all of the parents in the study stated that their children had access to computers at their schools. Staten Island elementary public school children are required to attend the school that is in the district in which they reside. Consequently, choosing schools whose students have access to computers was not a strategy that was intentionally utilized by the study parents. Parents interviewed described how their children had access to computers at home and in the public school setting. For 83% of the parents their children have also been given access to computers in other locations besides the home and public school setting such as a parent's gym or the public library. The study parents enabled their children to have access to computers in a multitude of settings.

Time to Interact with the Computer

For the parents present and guiding their children during the children's interaction with the computer, time was a way these parents offered their children access to computers. The various times the researcher observed the 6-year-old study children use home computers included after school, in the evening, on a Sunday morning, and in the early afternoon when there was a half day of school. The children were given time to interact independently with the computer and at other times to use the computer with their parents. During independent computer time the researcher observed as the children experimented and explored using computer hardware, software, and at times the Internet. A strategy that seemed to be used by all study parents was to allow the children to have time to access their home computer.

Withdrawal of Access to Video Games

During different times of the study, the issue of access to video games was discussed by parents of the 6-year-old boys. When the parent interviews were conducted, the parents of the three boys discussed the issue of video games. Parents of the three boys in the study mentioned how playing video games was limited at times or withheld as a reprimand. At the conclusion of one of the site visits, one mother was talking to the researcher and discussed her son's use of video games. During this discussion, this parent turned to her son and asked, "What do I use to punish you?" and the child's immediate response was a matter-of-fact, "No Game Boy." Withdrawal of personal computer access was *not* mentioned by any of the parents as a penalty for behavioral consequences. Therefore, a strategy that seemed to be used by all these parents was to make personal computer access available to their children without using the restriction of home computer use or access as a form of penalty or punishment.

Gender of Parent Guiding Children at the Computer

The parents guiding their 6-year-old children at the computer were both the mothers and the fathers of the participating families. Of the six families, there was one family with a mother as the head-of-household. The other five households were dual-parent families. The researcher observed and confirmed through video recordings that when a parent was guiding their child, either the father or mother provided assistance, but not both parents at the same time.

As presented in Figure 4.1, for Family 1 during site visit one and for Family 6 during site visit two, fathers guided their children at the computer. For the duration of the 24 home visits, these were the only two times when fathers guided their children at the computer, which equates to 8% of site visit time. The total percentage for all site visits when mothers were guiding their children at the computer was 92% of the time. A review of field notes and videotapes confirmed that the six mothers were the adults predominantly guiding their 6-year-old children at the computer. A possible reason for mothers being the parent to guide the children using the home computer could have been related to availability due to family schedules. Whether these mothers worked or went to college, the mothers were the parent who had the role of the adult who guided the child with the home computer.

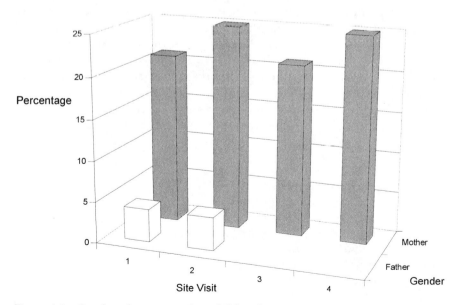

Figure 4.1   Gender of parent guiding child at the computer.

Language and Talk at the Computer

A strategy that all study parents utilized to guide their children's interaction with the home computer was talking with the children when the computer was being used. Talk focused on computer activity and computer challenges that occurred. The use of language as a strategy for parents guiding their children at the computer will be discussed further when research question two is considered.

Summary of Findings for Research Question One

For this qualitative/quantitative research study videotaped interviews of parents, study field notes, and videotaped parent-child interactions at the computer were carefully reviewed, transcribed, reviewed again, organized, interpreted, and reflected upon by this researcher. Through review of an array of data, research question one was explored: What strategies do these parents utilize to offer their children guidance and access to computers? One common theme that emerged from this study is that there were recurring approaches employed by parents when guiding their 6-year-old children using the home computer. These strategies included consistently offering assistance when children had a problem operating the computer hardware or software as well as moving within close proximity of a child in order to be of better assistance.

In the majority of the observed situations the mothers of the families offered assistance to the child. In an effort to offer their 6-year-old children access to computers, recurrent strategies employed by parents included having a computer in the home setting as well as enabling their children to access and utilize computers in other settings such as libraries or schools. Denying computer access to the children as a form of reprimand was not described as a parental approach for behavioral consequences by any of the parents in this study. Parents noted that their children's computer knowledge had grown and developed since the children's initial interaction with computers. Being offered time and opportunities to interact with computers was a strategy that these parents offered their children that may have contributed to the children's expanding computer knowledge.

RESEARCH QUESTION TWO

In this case study, discourse occurring at the computer was examined to be able to respond to research question two: What language categories and patterns do these parents utilize to guide their young children interacting with computers? Six parents were interviewed while being videotaped, 24 site visits were conducted, field notes were created, and parent-child interactions surrounding the computer were videotaped. Field notes were analyzed, videotapes transcribed, and data coded into the Mele Robinson Content Analysis Coding Sheet (see Appendix D). The purpose of the coding was to determine the types of language and discourse that were utilized by the parents while interacting with their children who were using a home computer. The categories generated after analyzing the transcriptions include adult language of parents talking to their children, talk between parents and the children, and nonverbal communications.

Methodology Utilized for the Analysis of Data for Research Question Two

The Mele Robinson Content Analysis Coding Sheet (see Appendix D) was a tool that was developed by this researcher to transfer transcription information into data in order to analyze verbal and nonverbal activity at the computer. Two aspects of talk were analyzed: adult language of what parents said to their children and the type of parent-child talk occurring at the computer. Verbal parental guidance of children at the computer was examined using adult language categories. The adult language coding analysis enabled the researcher to examine verbal communications and categorize instances when parents interacted with their child. Analysis included when a parent had a conversation with their child, asked their child a question, directed their child to perform a computer action without explanation, offered their child encouragement for computer actions taken, or gave their child an explanation for a computer action that was to be completed. The five adult language category groups were conversational language, inquiry language, directive language, validating language, and procedural language.

Videotaped sessions of talk at the computer also consisted of an analysis of discourse that took place between parents and their children interacting at a home computer. The element of computer software programs or web sites was not included as part of the analysis. The discourse between parent and child was grouped according to aspects of the talk occurring between the adult and child. Did the child, mother, or father initiate the talk? Did the father, mother, or child have a discussion about a topic? Was a question being asked by parent or child? Did a mother or father give their child feedback when the child made a statement? The discourse coding categories for talk between parents and their 6-year-old children were child initiated talk, mother initiated talk, father initiated talk, child inquiry, mother inquiry, father inquiry, or child discussion, mother discussion, father discussion as well as mother feedback or father feedback.

Table 4.7 represents a sample segment transcription with resulting discourse coding of talk, which occurred during a site visit observation of Family 2. As noted in coding results, both adult language categorization and parent-child talk at the computer are analyzed. After site visit videotapes were transcribed, incidences of parent and child discourse was coded and then frequency of occurrences counted. For example, for the discourse category

Table 4.7　Sample of Content Analysis Coding

Verbal/Nonverbal	Discourse Coding	Adult Language Categories	Comments
M: And then you get to choose if you want to go back again?	MI	IL	
M: Good idea.	MF	VL	
PJ: I already see two!	CD		
M: Okay. Excellent!	MD	CL	
M: Excellent.	MF	VL	
PJ: Oh man.	CD		
M: You found another one?	MI	IL	

Patrick Jr. = PJ
Mom = M

Discourse Codes
MI: Mother Inquiry
CI: Child Inquiry
MD: Mother Discussion
CD: Child Discussion
MR: Mother Response
MF: Mother Feedback

Adult Language Categories
CL: Conversational Language
IL: Inquiry Language
DL: Directive Language
VL: Validating Language
PL: Procedural Language

of inquiry, frequency counts were based on incidences when a participant initiated an inquiry, who responded to an inquiry, discussion between a mother or father and the participant child, and feedback that was given by parents. Nonverbal actions such as a child smiling or a parent pointing at the computer screen were also noted on the Mele Robinson Content Analysis Coding Sheet and were used during analysis to confirm validity of verbal findings. To respond to research question two the resulting content analysis coding was completed and categories tallied for frequency of occurrence to determine outcomes within and across parents and children.

Adult Language Category Coding

Adult language categories are related to communications used by parents when interacting with their children at the home computer. These categories emerged from the pilot study and were further refined for this more extensive study. In the pilot study the researcher's field notes and site visit videotapes documented that there was talk used by the parents that contained similar tones. Examples of such talk include a parent's voice elevating when asking a question or a parent's voice becoming slightly firmer in tone when giving their child a direction to complete a computer action. Word choices such as "Go there" or "Click on that" as a parent pointed to a computer screen were similar for the two parents of the pilot study.

This repetitive language was grouped into common categories. The groupings that emerged from the pilot study regarding adult language utilized by parents interacting with their children who were using the home computer were inquiry language, procedural language, validating language, and directive language. The adult language was categorized according to whether the parent's talk was asking the child a question, explaining the protocol to follow when using computer's hardware or software, offering their child positive verbal reinforcement for computer interactions, or directing the child's action with the computer.

After further review of data from the pilot study, an additional category emerged, that of conversational language. Conversational language was language utilized for discussion of a computer-related or social topic and did not fit into the other categories that had surfaced. The five adult language categories that emerged were inquiry language, directive language, validating language, procedural language, and conversational language.

According to Figure 4.2, the resulting total adult language categories for parents talking to their 6-year-old children at the computer varies for each adult language category. For parents talking to their children at the computer, 51% of adult language is conversational language (see Figure 4.2). Inquiry language was used by participant parents for 26% of the talk occurring during computer activity time. Parents verbally directed their children's actions with directive language for 18% of talk at the computer. Validating language and procedural language were used minimally at 4% and 1%

respectively. As noted in Figure 4.2, conversational language was the dominant adult language category used by parents during their children's activity
at the computer. A review of adult language categories and patterns that
emerged for each family and across families should assist in understanding
how these parents guided their children at the home computer.

Case Study Review and Adult Language Category Results

In order to better understand the types of language utilized by parents interacting with their children at a home computer, it is necessary to describe in
detail the different families and to give examples of the types of language
used by the participant parents in this study. The language utilized by all
parents was collected and Adult Language Categories tallied with parents
being considered as a whole group and also individually. The families in
this study were distinct and this classification of language utilized by adults
in each family merits further discussion.

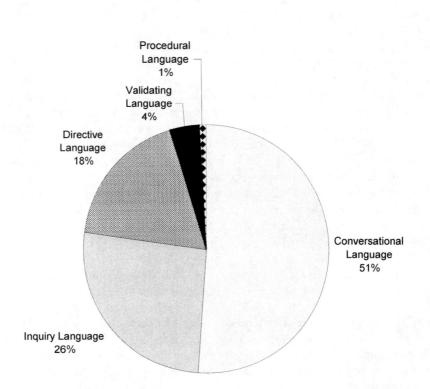

Figure 4.2   Adult language category totals for all parents and all site visits.

Family 1

The participants of Family 1 include 6-year-old Patrick Jr., his mother, and his father. Four site visits were done at this family's home, with field notes taken, and extensive videotaping, and transcribing of these videotapes completed. The home computer was located in the first-floor family room of the home. Patrick Jr.'s father, Patrick Sr., guided his son during the first site visit, on a Sunday. For the other three visits Patrick Sr. was not home when computer activity time was occurring during weekdays. Christina, Patrick Jr.'s mother, guided her son at the computer for these site visits.

When Patrick Jr. was at the computer during the four site visits, the parent interacting with him sat with him during his time at the home computer. During the researcher's first site visit Patrick Sr. sat next to his child on a chair within close proximity to his son. During the next three site visits Patrick Jr. was guided by his mother, Christina. She sat in a chair behind and slightly to the side of her son. During computer activity time Christina scrutinized the computer screen and watched her son's actions. During computer interaction Patrick Jr. interacted with both software game programs or parent approved child-oriented web sites. For Family 1 the parental proximity pattern that was observed was both parents were consistently within close proximity to their child. During computer activity timely responses were offered to questions from their son and both parents engaged in discussion with their child.

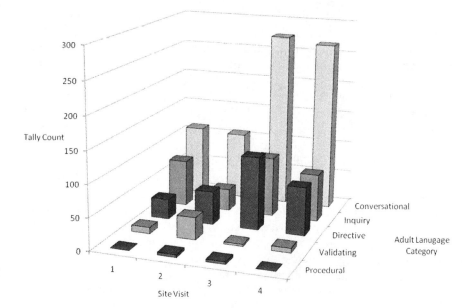

Figure 4.3 Family 1 frequency of adult language categories for site visits.

Figure 4.3 offers the frequency count totals for Family 1 of adult language categories used during activity at the home computer. Patrick, Jr. was guided by his father during the first site visit and his mother guided him during site visits two, three, and four. The dominant adult language category used by these parents when talking to their son was conversational language. As shown in Figure 4.3, the frequency count of conversational language was 111 occurrences for the first site visit, 107 for the second site visit, 275 for the third site visit, and 266 during the last site visit. Both Patrick Jr.'s mother and father talked to him often as he interacted with the home computer. The least occurring adult language category was procedural language, as these participant parents did not often explain to their child the technical reason for actions that needed to be taken when interacting with the computer hardware or software.

For Family 1, after converting the tally frequency count into percentages for adult language that was used, the most significant language category was conversational language. As shown in Figure 4.4, 55% of talk at the computer by Family 1 parents to their son was conversational language. Both directive language and inquiry language were approximately 20% of the talk used by these parents when they spoke to their child as he interacted with the home computer. There was only 4% of validating language used and 1% of procedural language used by these parents talking to their son at the computer during site visits.

Conversational language was the dominant adult language category used by Family 1 parents to their 6-year-old child (see Figure 4.4). Further analysis was considered to decide if conversational language was computer-related or social talk. Computer-related talk was discussion about activity occurring at the computer or focused on the computer. Social talk was discussion of non-related computer topics such as homework that needed to be done or a playdate the child had at another time. The analysis results revealed that 98% of Family 1 parents' conversational language to their child focused on computer-related discussion. Only 2% of talk at the computer was socially oriented. For this family, computer time was quality discussion time focused on computer activity for the parent participants and their child. Regardless of whether it was Patrick Jr.'s father or mother interacting with him at the computer, the parental pattern that was observed was that both of these parents appeared to offer their child their full visual and auditory attention.

Directive language, through which parents verbally direct their child's computer activity actions or reactions, was used for 20% of the talk by these parents when interacting with their child at the computer. When the adult language category percentages were ranked for all parent talk to their children at the computer during all site visits, Family 1 had the second highest percentage for the category of directive language compared to the other five families. For example, the directive language Patrick Sr. utilized included instructing his son to "always read before you click continue" or to "hold on." His mother would often guide Patrick Jr. to "click on here" or "see what that is" or to "give it (the computer screen changing) a minute." The language utilized by these parents suggests Patrick Jr.'s parents were attentive and involved with what their son was doing with the computer.

During the videotaped observation periods of Patrick Jr. interacting with the computer, Patrick Jr. led the focus of time at the computer by stating what activities he wanted to interact with. His parents both offered verbal support to allow him to interact and successfully engage with the chosen activity such as a computer game or an Internet web site. At times, Patrick Jr.'s parents would suggest alternative activities than the one the child had chosen. Then the parent and child would have a discussion and agree upon which activity would be chosen for time at the computer. Patrick Jr.'s parents would explain their reasons to their son, which included that the game chosen was now too easy for him or that his parents wanted Patrick Jr. to try another game that had more challenging levels the child had not tried yet.

Computer activity time when analyzed by reviewing field notes, videotapes, and transcriptions, appeared to be a cooperative activity between parents and child in Family 1. As presented in Figure 4.4, the language categories used most by parents in Family 1 were conversational language

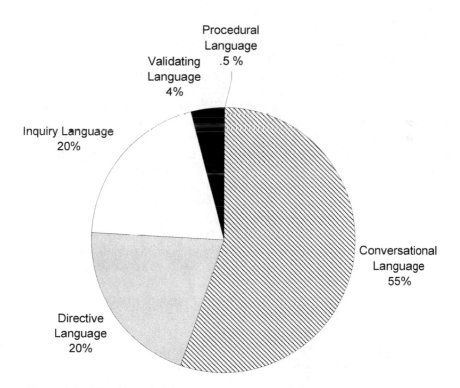

Figure 4.4 Family 1 adult language category totals for site visits.

(55%), directive language (20%), and inquiry language (20%) to guide their son at the computer. The patterns of behavior utilized by Patrick Sr. and Christina to guide their son included being in close proximity to their child while he was at the computer, offering verbal encouragement and guidance, and at times, directing their child's computer actions.

Family 2

The members of Family 2 included Victoria, the 6-year-old child, her 8-year-old brother, Joe, and their mother Elizabeth. This is a single-parent household and therefore the adult talk from parent to child observed in this household was between mother and child. Victoria's brother, Joe, was home for three of the site visits and did at times interact with his sister at the computer. Joe's involvement is not being discussed in study results as the focus for the current study is not siblings interacting at the computer. Four site visits were conducted at Victoria's house, field notes were taken, with extensive videotaping, and transcription of the resulting videotapes completed. The computer used during home site visits was the newer computer located in the dining room of the home.

For Family 2 the parental proximity pattern that was observed was that Victoria's mother was usually in general close proximity of 1–7 feet during the time the child was interacting with the computer. The frequency count totals of the adult language categories used by Victoria's mother, Elizabeth, during site visits is presented in Figure 4.5. The most frequently occurring adult language category used by this participant parent when talking to her child during every site visit was inquiry language (see Figure 4.5). During the first site visit the frequency count was 160 occurrences of inquiry language. During subsequent site visits the inquiry language frequency counts were 16, 69, and 8 respectively, which was the highest adult language category for this parent when talking to her daughter at the computer. Elizabeth would often ask Victoria questions such as, "Well what does it say on the bottom? What are your options?" or "What are you looking for now?"

The least frequently occurring adult language categories used by Elizabeth when talking to her child were both procedural language and validating language. Frequency counts for both adult language categories of procedural and validating language ranged from zero to five occurrences during all site visits (see Figure 4.5). This participant parent only occasionally explained to her daughter the reason for a course of action with the computer or offered positive verbal reinforcement to her child. Directive language, inquiry language, or conversational language was utilized more frequently than procedural language or validating language (see Figure 4.5).

During the first site visit, Victoria decided to play a software program entitled *Pajama Sam: No Need to Hide When it's Dark Outside.* This game had been given to Victoria by another family who no longer utilized it. During the first site visit, the *Pajama Sam* game was somewhat new to the child.

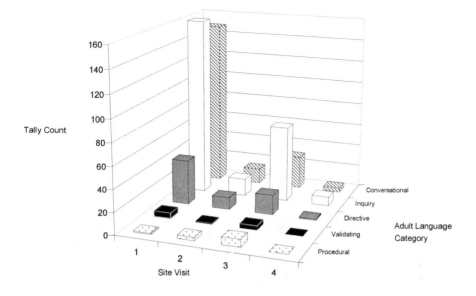

Figure 4.5   Family 2 frequency of adult language categories for site visits.

During site visit one, there was a higher proportion of both inquiry language and conversational language used by the parent than for any other home site visits (see Figure 4.5).

The mother of Family 2, Elizabeth, sat in close proximity to her daughter, Victoria, during the first site visit when the software program was new to this child. It was also the first visit of the researcher to this family. Therefore, it cannot be clearly ascertained whether parent time at the computer, proximity of parent to child, and type of language utilized were due to the new program or the novelty of a researcher visiting the home setting. Subsequent visits did not have as high a frequency count of 160 occurrences of adult inquiry language or 149 occurrences of adult conversational language (see Figure 4.5).

After determining all categories of adult language utilized during the four site visits for Family 2, the highest adult language category used by Elizabeth as she guided her daughter at the computer was the category of inquiry language with 47% of total parent talk (see Figure 4.6). The second highest adult language category used by Elizabeth when talking to her daughter, Victoria, was conversational language at 36% of parent talk. Elizabeth chatted with her daughter with talk focused on computer activity such as, "That's a pretty detailed game." There was also social language utilized by the parent participant not related to computer activity with comments such as "You're not even drinking your Shirley Temple and you made me make it." Inquiry language and conversational language

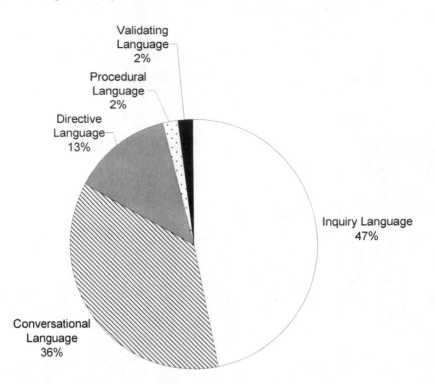

Figure 4.6   Family 2 adult language category totals for site visits.

were the two most frequently occurring adult language categories utilized overall by the adult participant. When further delving into the adult language category of conversational language for talk of Elizabeth to Victoria, it was revealed that 91% of the discussion by the participant parent was computer-related talk.

For the adult language category of inquiry language, a pattern was discerned from the qualitative data analysis of the language utilized by Elizabeth when talking to her child. This mother would ask her daughter two or three questions, without waiting for the child to respond to the questions asked. For example, during the *Pajama Sam* game, Elizabeth asked her daughter: "What about the mummy—the mummy there? Can you climb on him? Why can't you climb up on the bookshelf?" While the parent asked questions she would look at what her child was doing on the computer and seemed to assess what action needed to be taken. Sometimes the necessary action for the game required the use of the mouse. In that situation this mother would verbally direct her child from within a close proximity of approximately 2 feet and then the child completed the necessary action with the mouse. At other times, the parent moved physically closer to the child at the computer, took control of the mouse, and completed the action for the child. The pattern observed for this parent was to offer verbal directions and then either allow the child to complete the necessary action or the parent would maneuver the mouse to complete the action.

The language used by this mother to guide her child at the computer was asking questions, as well as discussing what was going on in the software program or possible ways to solve the game challenges. The parent would either tell the child what to do or would physically maneuver the software or computer equipment to solve computer questions that arose from her child regarding how to operate the hardware and software of the home computer. Not all computer glitches, such as a CD-ROM not working properly, were able to be solved by parent and child. With cooperative problem solving, such as selecting another CD-ROM, Elizabeth enabled Victoria to continue to have sustained interaction with their home computer.

Family 3

The family members for Family 3 include 6-year-old Samantha, her mother, Jean, her father, Daniel, and 4-year-old sister, Olivia. Both daughters were adopted from China and are not genetically related to each other. There were two home computers with one located in the dining room of the home and the other older computer located in the family room on the first floor of the home.

Four site visits were conducted at Samantha's home, field notes were taken, extensive videotaping done, and transcriptions of videotapes completed. During three of the visits her mother, Jean guided her daughter at the computer. For site visit three, Samantha's mother was at parent-teacher conferences when the researcher arrived. Samantha was going to be watched by her aunt. Her father was home but left shortly after the researcher arrived to meet Jean at Samantha's school. During this site visit Samantha interacted independently at the computer during the entire site visit. During the other three site visits, all family members were home, Samantha, her mother, her father, and younger sister. Samantha's father would occupy his younger daughter, Olivia, in another part of the home while Samantha was guided at the computer by her mother. The computer Samantha interacted with during all site visits was the newer computer located in the dining room on the second floor of the home. Samantha used software game programs during all site visits.

By considering the information from all site visits, Figure 4.7 represents the pattern of adult language categories that was revealed from the data collected and analyzed from home site visits. The frequency count of the adult language categories used by Jean, Samantha's mother, during the three site visits reveal that the most frequently occurring category used was conversational language. Occurrences of conversational language during site visits were 176, 197, and 54 respectively (see Figure 4.7).

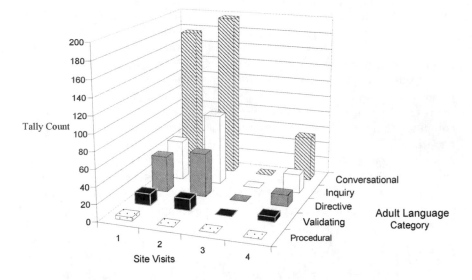

Figure 4.7   Family 3 frequency of adult language categories for site visits.

Samantha's mother, Jean, was consistent in the adult language categories chosen to guide her daughter. The ordinal rank of adult language categories for each visit remained in the same order with conversational language occurring most frequently, inquiry language second, directive language third, validating language fourth, and procedural language fifth. The frequency counts may have varied but the pattern of which adult language categories were used when this parent participant guided her child at the computer was consistent.

The highest occurring language category used by Jean was conversational language at 58% (see Figure 4.8). Parent talk was comprised of 21% inquiry language, 15% directive language, 5% validating language, and procedural language being 1% of parent talk to the child at the computer. The proportion of conversational language used by this mother, when ranked against the other parents in this study, was the highest for all the families in the study.

For conversational language used, the category was examined further to note whether the language was computer-related talk or social talk. In Figure 4.9 a comparison of the two subcategories of conversational language is revealed. Conversational language is compared to note if the adult language for parents in each family was computer-related talk or social language when having a conversation with their child at the computer.

When Jean had a discussion at the computer with her daughter, Samantha, 99% of the discussion was computer-related talk (see Figure 4.9). This participant parent would talk and discuss with her child the actions,

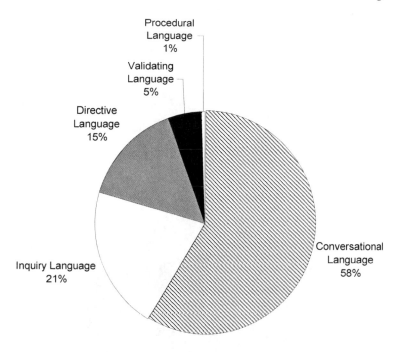

Figure 4.8   Family 3 adult language category totals for site visits.

choices, or activities happening in the game being played. Comments offered by Jean were in relation to information for a game or actions taken by Samantha. Examples of language utilized by Jean include "Oh you changed the music," "That says Enchanted Meadow," or "I think you did that one already." Social talk occurred when Samantha requested a drink or snack. Inquiry language was the second highest adult language category utilized by Jean. Examples of inquiry language used by Jean were "Why don't you color?" "What changes it from day to night? The fairy or the wand?" "Why don't you do the puzzle?"

Jean remained within close proximity of 2 to 4 feet from her daughter during most of Samantha's interaction with the computer. Jean attentively guided Samantha's interaction with selected software programs using directive language for 15% of her parent talk. Examples of directive language used by Jean to guide Samantha include "Click on no," "Go back to that tree branch," "Click to decorate," and "Type your name." An example of Jean guiding her daughter's selection of software game interaction includes "Do you want to do the Buzz Lightyear one? I think this is sort of a junk game but let's take a look . . . this says educational, so let's see what's there. Puzzle. Living letters." Jean would stand next to her daughter and would read game directions or information as needed to guide her daughter to be able to continue to interact with the game selected.

The patterns that emerged with regard to Jean's interactions with her daughter during the videotaped time at the computer were that this mother guided her young child by being within close proximity to the child and the home computer. Also, this mother had the pattern of talking to her daughter often about what was happening on the computer screen for the game selected. Jean, Samantha's mother, frequently offered suggestions with 15% of parent talk being directive language to guide her child's actions and reactions to the game activity. Adult language categories utilized by Jean mainly included 58% conversational language, 21% inquiry language, and 15% directive language.

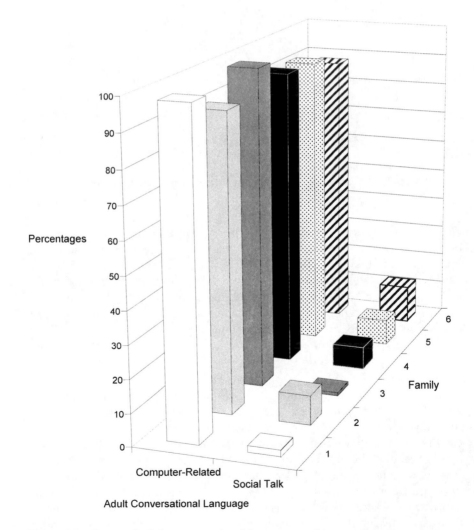

Figure 4.9   Focus of adult conversational language at the computer.

Family 4

The family members of Family 4 include 6-year-old Ashley, her mother, Gina, her father, and 8-year-old brother, Christopher. While Ashley's father resides in the household, he was at work and not present during any of the site visits. Four site visits were completed at Ashley's house, field notes were taken, and extensive videotapes were recorded and transcribed. The home computer is located in the parents' bedroom of this one-floor home.

Gina guided her 6-year-old daughter Ashley with the computer during the videotaped site visits. The frequency count of the adult language categories used by this mother during the site visits is presented in Figure 4.10. The adult language category occurring most often by Gina in three of the four visits was conversational language. The frequency count for conversational language was 88 occurrences during the first site visit, 18 occurrences during site visit two, eight during the third visit, and 27 occurrences during the fourth site visit.

During the first visit Gina was showing her daughter how to use an educational web site that was new to the child. This participant parent sat next to her child on a chair for most of the visit and guided Ashley as she interacted with the chosen game activity. Gina explained to her daughter how to use the game activity and verbally guided her child's interaction

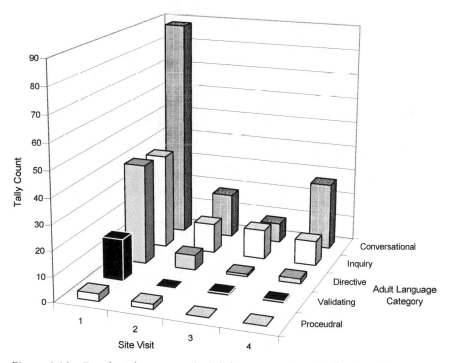

Figure 4.10   Family 4 frequency of adult language categories for site visits.

with the web site. During the first site visit, talk used by this mother had more occurrences in each of the adult language categories than for any of the other observations of this family. An example of the higher frequency of occurrences for adult language during the first site visit compared to other visits was that there were 40 occurrences of directive language during the first site visit with only six occurrences during the second visit, one during the third visit, and two occurrences during the last visit.

For parent talk of Gina to her daughter, Ashley, 65% of all talk occurred during the first site visit. For the adult language category of validating language, 89% of occurrences for this language category occurred during this site visit. Validating language used by Gina especially during the first site visit included "Yeah! You got 17 out of 17, way to go! Good job!", "You're smart," and "Very good." Ashley seemed pleased when given praise by her mother and responded with "Thanks" or a giggle. Through Figure 4.11, a comparison of Gina's talk to her daughter during all site visits can be examined. The most frequently occurring talk was conversational language (49%). Inquiry language (25%) and directive language (17%) were used less frequently. Validating language (7%) and procedural language (2%) were the least frequently occurring categories of parent talk.

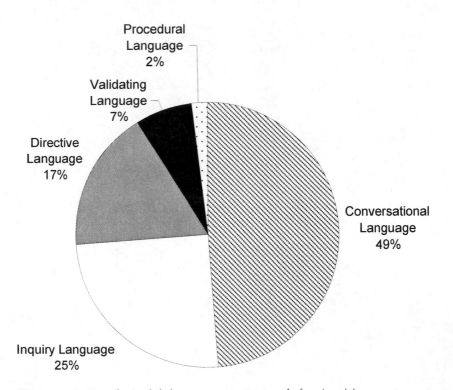

Figure 4.11   Family 4 adult language category totals for site visits.

After analyzing the transcripts and reviewing the videotapes, it is hypothesized by this researcher that since this mother introduced her child to a new web site and activity, this could be the reason for the higher proportion of talk and positive reinforcement during the first site visit. This high statistic might also be due to the presence of the researcher for the first time in the home. The reason for the higher proportion of talk and positive feedback during site visit one cannot be precisely determined. The resulting impact on the child was being able to learn about how to interact with the game offered on a new web site.

Overall, during the four site visits almost half of the parent talk was conversational language when Gina talked to her daughter Ashley. When examining the adult language category of conversational language, computer-related discussion was used 93% of the time. Examples of conversational language used by Gina include "We're doing options, let's see what other things there are to do," "So we'll do easy," or "I know, the mouse is giving me a hard time today too." The language used by Gina focused on what was going on with the computer activity for the majority of discussion occurring at the computer.

In this particular observational site, it is important to note that the home telephone is linked to the computer. During site visits one and two, an educational web site was used for the child to interact with a game. Accepting an incoming telephone call would have interrupted computer activity time. At the end of site visit two Gina actually said, "We're gonna shut it down. And the phone didn't even ring once! I'm shocked! Wow, I'm shocked!" If a telephone call was expected, a decision would need to be made about whether or not to continue access to the Internet or use the family cellular telephone to receive incoming calls.

As previously mentioned, during the first site visit Gina sat with her daughter as she was introduced to a new Internet activity. On visit two the child used the web site again and was familiar with the activity. For the second and subsequent visits this mother made sure her child accessed the web site she desired then the mother left the computer area. She would be in another room of the home such as the kitchen or living room. When Ashley called, "Mom!" she would respond, "Yes" or "What do you need, honey?" and would consistently return to the room to assist her daughter. Whenever Ashley called her mother the response would be inquiry language such as, "What's up?" "What's the matter, honey?" or "Do you need my help?" A pattern that this parent used to guide her child was to verbally respond to requests for assistance and then always come within close proximity of 2 to 3 feet to the child, to assist with solving the program or hardware challenge.

The adult language categories utilized by this parent were mainly conversational language and inquiry language. Gina used directive language for 17% of talk and validating language for 7% of parent talk to guide her daughter as she interacted with the home computer. The adult language categories utilized and proximity to the child participant varied during these site visits and it is hypothesized that this is related to the child's level of familiarity with the computer task. When the task was new, there was more language between the child and parent participant and a closer proximity between parent and child. Once the child's familiarity with the web site grew, the use of language declined and proximity diminished. Being responsive verbally and coming in closer proximity when her daughter verbally asked for computer assistance was a pattern utilized by this parent.

Family 5

Family members for Family 5 include 6-year-old Eric, his mother, Aileen, his sister Jaime, and his father. Eric's father resides in the household and was at work during site visits. The participants of this study were Aileen and Eric. For three of the site visits Eric's sister, Jaime, was in the household but was occupied with other activities and did not interact with Eric at the home computer. Aileen would often be in the general area as her son interacted with the home computer. The computer was located in the dining room on a desk and Aileen would be in the kitchen, living room, or at times on the second floor of the home.

The frequency count of the adult language categories used during site visits by Aileen, Eric's mother, is presented in Figure 4.12. For Aileen's talk to her son, the adult language category of conversational language had the most occurrences for parent talk. There were 20 occurrences of conversational

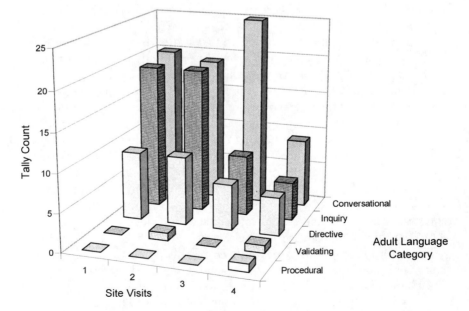

Figure 4.12   Family 5 frequency of adult language categories for site visits.

language during the first site visit, 19 during site visit two, 25 during site visit three, and 9 occurrences during site visit four. Inquiry language was the second highest adult language category when Aileen talked to her son at the computer. For both procedural language and validating language, there was one or zero occurrences during all site visits (see Figure 4.12).

All categories were determined for the four site visits for Family 5, and as shown in Figure 4.13, the highest occurring adult language category was conversational language with 46% of parent talk. Inquiry language occurred for 33% of Aileen's talk to her son, Eric, during his computer activity time. A more in-depth examination of Aileen's conversational language reveals that 92% of the adult conversational talk was computer-related.

Aileen would assist her son when the home computer hardware or software had a glitch or a web site did not function properly. For example, when Eric had difficulty trying to type the information to access a web site, his mother verbally told him what letters to type to be able to access the site. If the computer was not allowing Eric to access AOL, Aileen would move in close proximity to the home computer and type in information to try to access AOL for Eric. If Eric verbally asked for

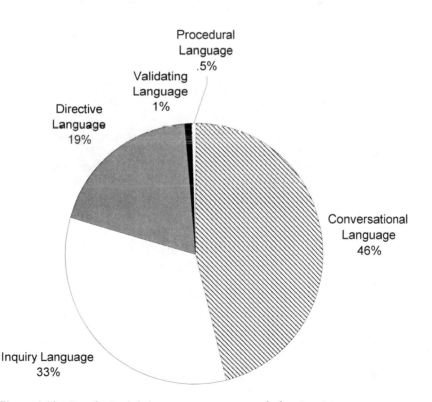

Figure 4.13   Family 5 adult language category totals for site visits.

assistance when trying to use a software program that would not operate properly, his mother would check to see if the CD-ROM was scratched. At times when Eric did encounter what appeared to the researcher to be a software or web site difficulty, he would independently resolve the computer software problem or explore a different game or activity on the web site.

One notable pattern of behavior exhibited by this mother that became evident during data analysis was Aileen's method of guidance given to her son as he interacted with the home computer. As she worked around the home this mother would periodically ask her son about his activities as he interacted with a software game or web site activity. Examples of inquiry language Aileen would use when checking on her son's computer activity include "What are you playing," "How are you doing," or "You having a problem there?" She also would periodically check on her son's activity visually as she passed through the area where he was using the computer. Although this parent might have been in another room or floor of the house, and might not have always been in close proximity to her child, she would check her son's computer interaction regularly. The patterns that emerged with regard to Aileen guiding her son with the computer included checking on his activity and, when needed, being within close proximity to offer guidance.

QUANTITY OF PARENT TALK

It is hypothesized by this researcher from review and analysis of field notes, videotapes, and transcriptions, that the resulting quantity of talk by this parent to her child is impacted by her not being in close proximity. The quantity of parent talk for this participant parent was significantly less than for families with parents who usually remained in general close proximity of 7 feet or less to their child during computer activity time. For Families 1, 2, and 3 a parent was usually within close proximity while their children interacted with the home computer. For Family 1, totals for occurrences of adult language were 1,607. For Family 2, occurrences of parent talk totaled 553, and for Family 3, occurrences of parent talk were 733. When the quantity of adult talk for each family is totaled and then compared to each other, the resulting percentages offer a comparison of quantity of parent talk. When compared to Family 1, with a proportion of 46% of the total parent talk, which is the highest occurrence of a parent talking to their child at the computer, Aileen of Family 5 comprised only 5% of the total parent talk at the computer. A statistical analysis of the transcriptions indicates that conversational language occurred for 49% of parent talk, inquiry language occurred for 32% of parent talk, directive language for 19% of parent talk, with validating and procedural language being minimal at 1% or less respectively.

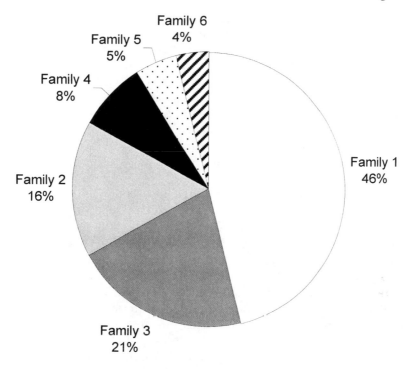

Figure 4.14   Comparison of quantity of parent talk.

Family 6

Family members for Family 6 included 6-year-old Kyle, his mother Barbara, his father Michael, and his brother Joseph. There were four site visits conducted at this family's home with field notes taken, extensive videotapes recorded, and transcribing of these videotapes completed. Kyle's mother was home during all four site visits. Kyle's father was home and available to assist his son during the second site visit but was either not home or not available to assist during the other three site visits. During the second site visit either Kyle's mother or father offered assistance when he needed guidance with the computer. The home computer was located in the den on the first floor of their house.

Barbara, Kyle's mother, was the parent who mainly was available to guide her 6-year-old son at the home computer. Kyle usually interacted at the computer independently, with his favorite activity being a Godzilla web site. The Godzilla science-fictional character was one of Kyle's favorite interests at this time, with his computer activity time choice being the Godzilla web site with Godzilla videotapes and Godzilla action figures. Kyle's father shared with the researcher that as a child he too was interested in the Godzilla character. As Kyle interacted with the Godzilla web site he would select and listen to sound bites of the monster making growling noises or watch short action video clips of Godzilla.

As seen in Figure 4.15, procedural language and validating language were not used at all by either parent during any site visits. During the first site visit this participant mother, Barbara, asked her son, Kyle, if he wanted a drink. She then left the area and went to the second floor of their home. Kyle did not appear to need any assistance with his computer activity as he independently logged on and then interacted with a Godzilla web site. Kyle did not call for his mother at any time for assistance during this visit. During the four visits Kyle's mother, Barbara, was usually not-in-close proximity when the child was interacting with the home computer.

During the second site visit Kyle's father was present for the beginning of the time Kyle was at the computer. His mother was home during the entire time Kyle was interacting with the computer. The second site visit began with Barbara telling her son Kyle "Okay, I'm going upstairs if you need anything, shout." During this site visit observation when Kyle needed assistance, he called either his father or mother. To be able to assist their son, these participant parents offered an immediate verbal response to their child and then followed up by physically moving within closer proximity to their child. Actions taken to be able to assist Kyle included his father walking over to the computer or his mother coming from another floor to be within closer proximity to the child and computer. A pattern used by

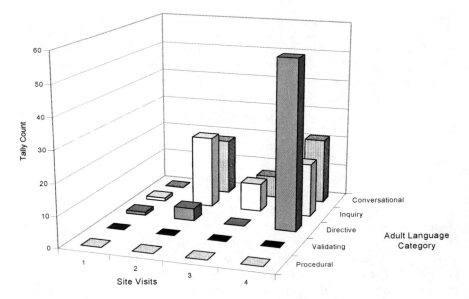

Figure 4.15   Family 6 frequency of adult language categories for site visits.

these parents was to be within 5-foot proximity when offering their son assistance with computer difficulties encountered.

During site visit four Kyle had a problem trying to get a CD-ROM software program disk to be read by the computer. Kyle called to his mother for assistance as he wanted to play a game on the CD-ROM. Ninety-two percent of the directive language that occurred during all site visits transpired as Barbara was trying to get the CD-ROM to work properly. The overall directive language percentage of 38% (see Figure 4.16) is skewed by the higher proportion of directive language used during site visit four, as Barbara tried to get the nonfunctioning CD-ROM to work properly. Eventually the CD-ROM would not function and the child chose another activity.

A statistical analysis of the transcriptions indicates that inquiry language was 32% of parent talk, the second highest adult language category (see Figure 4.16). Examples of inquiry language used by Kyle's mother were often clarifying questions such as "What do you want me to do, honey?" or "What's the

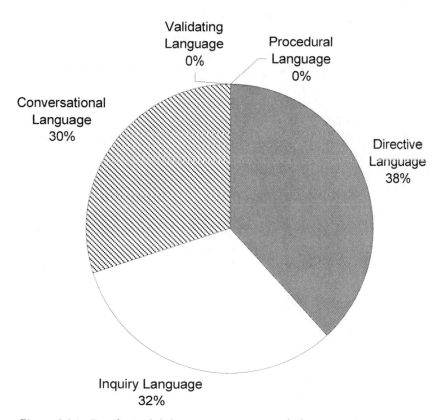

Figure 4.16   Family 6 adult language category totals for site visits.

matter?" His mother, who was at home during the majority of the site visits, was often not in the area while her son was interacting with the computer.

Conversational language was 30% of parent talk. Upon closer examination of conversational language, it was revealed that 12% was social language. An example of social talk included Barbara asking Kyle if he wanted a drink or some water. For Family 6 parents, computer-related talk was 88%, which is the lowest for all the study families. The level of computer-related talk did not appear to have a negative impact on Kyle's computer interaction as he was able to independently use the computer during most of the site visits. At times when his parents could not resolve a computer problem, such as when the CD-ROM malfunction could not be corrected, Kyle would select another activity and would continue interacting with the computer. The data analysis did reveal the use of adult language categories for Family 6 as being 38% directive language for parent talk, 32% inquiry language, and 30% conversational language for parent talk to their child at the home computer. Family 6 parents guided their son during time at the computer by offering support when the child requested assistance.

Common Characteristics across Parents for Adult Language Categories

Six families were selected and studied for this qualitative/quantitative study about the interactions of parents with their 6-year-old children while the children were utilizing a home computer. Data collected included field notes, videotaped parent interviews, and four videotaped site visits for each of the six families. After carefully analyzing data, it was determined that language was a significant tool used by the parents in this study as a strategy for guiding their 6-year-old children interacting with a home computer. Verbal support was offered by the parents when their children were interacting with a software program or browsing an approved online web site.

Through analysis of the adult language categories for each site visit for every parent, the rank order of the most frequently occurring adult language categories ascending to the least frequently used language categories was calculated. Among the parent participants in this study conversational language was one of the top two ranked categories for all six families. Figure 4.9 portrays data in percentages across parents when conversational language focused on primarily computer-related talk used by participant parents to their children. The percentage of computer-related conversational language discussion ranged from 88% for Family 6 to 99% for Family 3 (see Figure 4.9). A language category that was used minimally by participant parents was procedural language to explain why a certain computer action needed to be initiated or what the function was of certain computer hardware. Figure 4.2 confirms that at 1% of parent talk, procedural language was the least occurring adult language category.

Another common pattern that was observed among all participant parents to guide their children at the computer was to be in close proximity when offering computer assistance. In this study there were six families and seven parent participants. Three of the parent participants out of the seven parent participants chose to remain in the immediate area near the computer while their children were interacting with the home computer. The researcher observed that the other four parent participants seemed to be occupied with household duties and did not remain in the immediate area near their child and the computer.

Both groups of parents, those in close proximity and those parents not-in-close proximity to their child at the home computer, were consistent in verbally responding every time their children verbally asked a question or needed assistance with the computer. The consistency of participant parents responding to their children verbally and then physically moving in closer proximity to assist their child at the home computer was a pattern exhibited by every participant parent.

Parent-Child Discourse Coding

In addition to focusing on and analyzing the language utilized only by parent participants while their children were at the home computer, discourse between participant parents and their 6-year-old children was examined. The videotapes from site visits were transcribed and analysis was accomplished using the Mele Robinson Content Analysis Coding classifications. These transcriptions contained talk of who asked a question, who responded to a question, who offered discussion, and parents' verbal feedback to their children. The discourse coding categories utilized were: child inquiry, mother inquiry, father inquiry, child discussion, mother discussion, father discussion, child response, mother response, father response, mother feedback, or father feedback. The procedure for coding discourse included the following classifications: inquiry (I), discussion (D), response (R), and feedback (F) which will be referred to as the IqDRF format. The coding for study participants was for the child (C), mother (M), or father (F). As the coding was analyzed, the categories of mother and father were also considered by combining the two distinct categories of mother and father into the one combined category of parents (P). The resulting occurrences of discourse between participant parents and their children were coded and then tally counts for frequency of occurrences were completed.

The coding of discourse enabled talk for each site visit and for every study participant to be analyzed. The results of analysis for frequency counts for each participant category offered category totals for mother inquiry (MI), child inquiry (CI), mother discussion (MD), and child discussion (CD). The resulting frequency count, of discourse at the computer between mothers or fathers and their children, was considered with the separate category groupings of mothers or fathers.

Examining the categories of discourse for mothers and fathers as separate categories did not reveal significant discourse patterns or themes. When the separate categories of mother and father were merged for analysis purposes into the combined category of parents, the size of the frequency count for the merged category of participant parents became more significant. The systematic coding of transcripts enabled analysis of data to respond to research question two for language categories and patterns that the seven participant parents employed to guide their 6-year-old children interacting with computers.

Discourse Coding Results

Six families were each visited four times by the researcher. Data in the form of field notes and videotaping of parents and children interacting with the home computer were collected. The study data were methodically coded and subsequently analyzed to unveil the talk occurring between participant parents and their 6-year-old children at the home computer. In this study discourse coding categories were utilized to examine the discourse of parents talking to their children. Through the use of discourse coding categories, the coding revealed who asked a question, who responded, who discussed a topic, and the adult who offered feedback to a child. The results of the discourse coding are described in terms of discussion between participant parents and their 6-year-old children.

Parent-Child Discussion

For this study, parent-child discourse was considered to be talk between a parent and his or her child. There were six families with six 6-year-old children and seven parent participants included in this study. Analyses of videotape transcriptions resulted in discourse coding of parent-child talk. For Families 1, 2, 3, and 4 the two largest categories of discourse occurring during computer activity time were parent discussion and child discussion. For Family 5, the two largest discourse categories was parent discussion first and parent inquiry second. For Family 6, the two largest discourse coding categories were analyzed to be parent inquiry first and parent discussion second.

Overall, when scrutinizing the discourse coding totals for all families and all four site visits, the resulting analysis reveals that the two main discourse coding categories were 31% parent discussion and 30% child discussion (see Figure 4.17). The total percentage of these two main categories for parent-child discussion was 61% of discourse occurring when the 6-year-old children were guided by their participant parents at a home computer. Parent discussion, at 31% of talk, is the discourse category that best correlates to the adult language category of conversational language, at 51%. As noted in both the analysis of adult language categories and parent-child discourse coding categories of talk at the computer, study parents talk to their children often during computer activity time. Subsequently, the largest

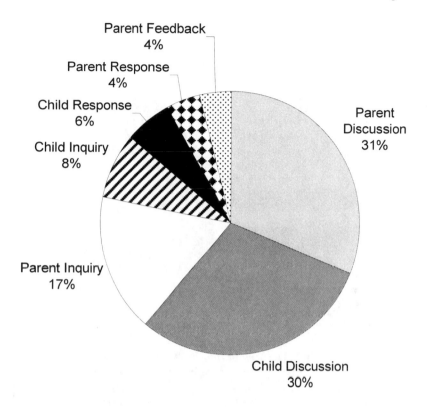

Figure 4.17 Discourse coding totals for all families and all site visits.

discourse category for the 6-year-old study children was 30% being child discussion. Talking at the computer was evident as a strategy for parents when guiding their children at the computer as well as a characteristic for parents and children during activity at the computer.

Upon further analysis for the discourse category of child discussion, it is noted that there are fewer occurrences of child discussion for the 6-year-old children in Families 4, 5, and 6 than there are for the children in Families 1, 2, and 3 (see Figure 4.18). Analysis of the researcher's field notes, along with review of site visit videotapes discloses that the participant parents for Families 1, 2, and 3 were within 7 feet from where their children and the computer were located. The parents of Families 4, 5, and 6 were not consistently in the area where their children and the computer were located but were often 8 or more feet away from their child and the home computer. This researcher is hypothesizing that the differences in quantity for the discourse category of child discussion could possibly be due to proximity of parents to their children during computer activity time; the difference may be gender related as two out of the three boys had less discussion

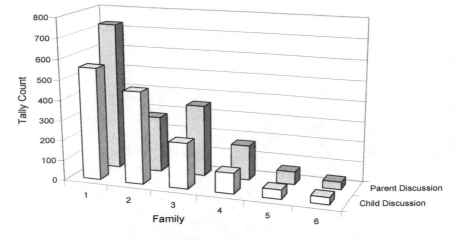

Figure 4.18   Frequency of parent and child discussion for each family.

than the other participant children, or the difference in fewer occurrences of discourse between parents and their children for Families 4, 5, and 6 may be due to chance. Further studies are needed to determine which factor might be most influential to the increased level of discussion.

For Families 1, 2, and 3 parents remained in the area where their children were interacting with a home computer. When the discourse categories of parent discussion and child discussion were combined for Family 1, the results indicate that total parent-child discussion was 65% of discourse that occurred during talk at the computer. For Family 3, when the categories of parent discussion and child discussion are combined, the result is that 62% of discourse at the computer is parent-child discussion. The combined parent-child discussion categories for Family 2 totaled 58% of discourse occurring at the computer. The lower combined percentage for the parent-child discussion category for Family 2, as compared to Family 1 or Family 3, may be related to the number of occurrences when the child was talking to herself during her interaction with the home computer.

Victoria, the 6-year-old child of Family 2, would at times talk aloud as she interacted with computer software games or tried to resolve a computer game challenge. According to the researcher's field notes and from review of the videotapes, Victoria did not appear to always be talking to her mother or talking with an expectation of getting a response. An example of Victoria's self talk is when she was interacting with the computer to play the *Pajama Sam* software computer game. Victoria looked at the computer screen and said, "There's a sock up there. We need the rope, but how? I'm going to eat something (as a way to try to solve the game dilemma), I can't find anything." This child's self-talk approach to computer interaction resulted in the discourse category of child discussion being 36% and the combined categories of parent-child discussion being 58% of parent-child talk at the computer (see Figure 4.19). Victoria's discourse category of child discussion (36%) was the highest child discussion percentage for all participant children in this study.

For Family 2, parent discussion was 22% of discourse, which was the lowest percentage of parent discussion for all participant parents. It is hypothesized by this researcher that the child discussion category of discourse was the highest for this participant child and the parent discussion category of discourse the lowest as a result of Victoria's self talk at the computer. Parent and child discussion as the main categories for discourse at the computer was a theme that emerged from the collection and analysis of field notes, videotapes, and site observation transcriptions. The data uncovered the quantity of parent-child discussion and subsequent percentages of discussion for participant parents and their children interacting at the home computer. For example, 61% of discourse occurring at the computer for all study participants for all site visits was parent-child discussion. The proximity of participant parents to their 6-year-old

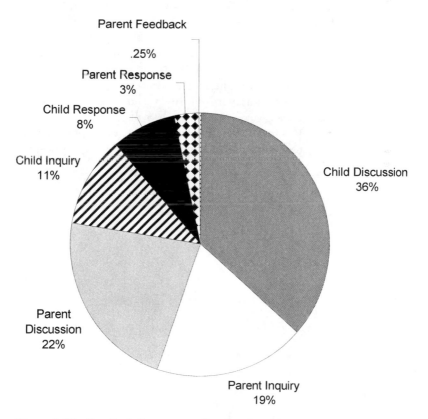

Figure 4.19   Family 2 discourse coding for site visits.

children interacting with a home computer affected the quantity of parent-child discourse.

Parent-Child Discourse Pattern and Proximity

Parent-child discourse patterns can be described as arrangements of discourse coding categories that repeat within participant parents and their 6-year-old children or across participant families in this study. The videotaped site visits were reviewed, transcribed, and analyzed using Mele Robinson Content Analysis Coding categorization. The talk occurring at the computer for every participant parent and their 6-year-old children was scrutinized to appraise the discourse coding categories and frequency of occurrences for parent-child talk at the home computer.

Methodical examination of the coding data uncovered recurring discourse coding category rank order for participant parents and their 6-year-old children. In Table 4.8 the total discourse coding percentages for all site visits and all study participants are ranked from the highest frequency percentages being ranked at 1 and the lowest at 7. The resulting pattern that emerges for Family 1 and Family 3 is identical. The coding sequence for both Family 1 and Family 3 is PD-CD-PI-CI-CR-PR-PF which equates to: parent discussion (PD), child discussion (CD), parent inquiry (PI), child inquiry (CI), child response (CR), parent response (PR), and parent feedback (PF). For Family 1 and Family 3, in the entire sequence of discourse coding categories, from highest to lowest, rank order is the same. The top two rank order categories for Family 1 and Family 3 were parent discussion and child discussion. The participant parents of Family 1 and Family 3 were within 3–4 feet of their children for the most part during the time their children interacted with a home computer. It is hypothesized by

Table 4.8   Rank Order by Percentage of Discourse Coding Category Totals

	Rank Order						
	1	2	3	4	5	6	7
Family 1	PD	CD	PI	CI	CR	PR	PF
Family 2	CD	PD	PI	CI	CR	PR	PF
Family 3	PD	CD	PI	CI	CR	PR	PF
Family 4	PD	CD	PI	CR	CI	PF	PR
Family 5	PD	PI	CD	CR	CI	PR	PF
Family 6	PI	PD	CD	CR	CI	PR	PF

Note:
Discourse Codes

PI=Parent Inquiry	PR=Parent Response
CI=Child Inquiry	CR=Child Response
PD=Parent Discussion	PF=Parent Feedback
CD=Child Discussion	

this researcher that the close proximity of parents to their children, while being verbally and physically engaged in their child's task on the computer, resulted in the quantity of parent discussion and child discussion being the two highest ranking discourse coding categories for Family 1 and Family 3.

For Family 2 the highest rank order discourse category was child discussion and the second highest was parent discussion. Six-year-old Victoria of Family 2 is the participant child who talked aloud while she interacted with the home computer. The rank order for the two highest ranked discourse categories for Family 2 is similar to the discourse category rank order results for Family 1 and Family 3. For Family 1 and Family 3 the rank order from highest to lowest for discourse categories is PD first and CD second. For Family 2 the rank order of discourse coding categories from highest to lowest is CD first and PD second. The discourse coding categories of CD and PD for Family 2 are the same categories as for Family 1 and Family 3 but with the rank order reversed. The remaining rank order of discourse categories for Family 1, Family 2, and Family 3 are in the same descending sequence with rank order positions from high to low being PI-CI-CR-PR-PF which equates to parent inquiry, child inquiry, child response, parent response, and parent feedback.

In Table 4.9 examination and analysis of the discourse coding for participant parents and their children resulted in frequency counts and subsequently rank order calculations that present the rank order pattern are noted. The participant parents of Family 1, Family 2, and Family 3 remained within general close proximity or close proximity to their 6-year-old children for the majority of time while the participant children were using the home computer. Parent discussion and child discussion were the two highest discourse categories. The third and fourth highest ranked discourse categories that occurred most often for Family 1, Family 2, and Family 3 were parent inquiry and child inquiry. The fifth and sixth rank ordered discourse categories were child response and parent response. The lowest occurring rank order discourse category for Family 1, Family 2, and Family 3 was the discourse category of parent feedback.

The significance of the rank order results is that discussion was the priority discourse category when the participant parents and participant children of Family 1, Family 2, and Family 3 interacted together at the home computer. Talking about what was occurring on the computer screen for a software game, solving challenges of how to interact with an Internet web site, or talking about how to use the computer's hardware were observed by the researcher during parent-child discussions that occurred. Parents and children asking questions, with children and parents responding to those questions, seemed to be the approach used by participant families.

For Families 5 and 6 participant parents did not remain in close proximity during computer time, with the resulting parent inquiry discourse category results being 21% and 30% respectively. For the 6-year-old boys of Family 5 and Family 6, when the children verbally asked for computer

Table 4.9 Rank Order by Percentage of Adult Language Categories for All Visits

	Site Visit 1	Site Visit 2	Site Visit 3	Site Visit 4
Family 1	CL	CL	CL	CL
	IL	DL	DL	DL
	DL	IL	IL	IL
	VL	VL	VL	VL
	PL	PL	PL	PL
Family 2	IL	IL	IL	IL
	CL	CL	CL	CL
	DL	DL	DL	DL
	VL	VL	VL	VL
Family 3	CL	CL	CL	CL
	IL	IL	—	IL
	DL	DL	—	DL
	VL	VL	—	VL
	PL	PL	—	PL

Family 4			
CL	CL	CL	CL
DL	IL	IL	IL
IL	DL	DL	DL
VL	PL	PL	VL
PL	VL	VL	PL

Family 5			
CL	CL	CL	CL
IL	IL	IL	IL
DL	DL	DL	DL
PL	VL	PL	PL
VL	PL	VL	VL

Family 6			
IL	IL	IL	DL
DL	CL	CL	CL
CL	DL	DL	IL
VL	PL	PL	PL
PL	VL	VL	VL

Language Categories:
CL: Conversational Language   DL: Directive Language
IL: Inquiry Language   PL: Procedural Language
VL: Validating Language

assistance, questions had to be asked by participant parents to assess what assistance or guidance was needed. Through review of videotapes this researcher noted that for these two children, a pattern emerged: as proximity decreased, the need to ask questions increased. For Family 6, 30% of the discourse occurring at the computer was parent-inquiry. For Family 6, the participant parent was often in another room or on another floor of the house as her 6-year-old child interacted with the home computer. Barbara, Kyle's mother, usually asked her son a question after he called for assistance with the computer. For the participant child of Family 6, guidance was offered when the child requested assistance with the computer. From review of videotapes, transcriptions, and field notes, this researcher hypothesizes that the proximity of participant parents to their 6-year-old children interacting with a home computer had an impact on the level of parent inquiry needed for participant parents to be able to offer their child guidance resolving computer challenges.

Summary of Findings for Research Question Two

Examination of adult language used by parents and discourse coding of talk between parents and their children enabled consideration of research question two: What language categories and patterns do these parents utilize to guide their young children interacting with computers? The study results found that the adult language categories of participant parents talking to their 6-year-old children consisted of mostly conversational language (51%). All participant parents' conversational language was examined further and the distinction was established between social talk and computer-related conversational language. It was revealed that 96% of all adult conversational language was computer-related. Through the use of conversational language which focused on computer-related discussion, participant parents were able to guide their children during computer interaction.

When the discourse category totals are considered for all site visits and all parent-child discourse, the discourse category of discussion emerges as the largest category. When the discourse categories of parent discussion (31%) and child discussion (30%) are combined the discourse category of discussion (61%) is revealed as the dominant discourse category. The subsequent categories are parent inquiry (17%), with child inquiry, parent response, child response, and parent feedback all being below 10% of total discourse occurring for parent-child interaction at the computer. The result of parent-child discourse in the use of discussion was dominant with fluid talk occurring at the computer which enabled participant parents to guide their 6-year-old children at the computer. Study parents demonstrated the characteristics of being consistent in responding to their children and being within close proximity when offering their children guidance.

RESEARCH QUESTION THREE

The third research question of the current study is: What do these parents consider the significance of computers in their children's lives and what are common goals for their children's acquisition of computer knowledge? To respond to this research question, data were collected in several ways: parent interviews, researcher observations, field notes, and videotaped home site visits. Videotaped parent interviews and site visits were transcribed and analyzed with field notes scrutinized. The third research question is addressed by considering (a) what these parents consider the significance of computers in their children's lives and (b) common goals these parents have for their children's acquisition of computer knowledge.

Methodology Utilized for the Analysis of Data for Research Question Three

Parent interviews were conducted for participant parents using questions from the Parent Computer Perspective Interview (see Appendix B). The resulting parent interview videotapes were transcribed and analyzed for recurrent word choices or themes that emerged from parent responses. Videotaped site visits were reviewed for participant parents' verbal and non-verbal activity with their participant children interacting with the home computer. Field notes were reviewed to offer additional information which might not have been available on the video camera recordings. The resulting descriptive qualitative data revealed participant parents' perspectives and goals with computers for their 6-year-old children.

Significance of Computers

The researcher conducted parent interviews using the Parent Computer Perspective Interview which consisted of 20 questions that were asked of one parent from each participating study family. The interview questions were employed to obtain information about parental perspectives for interview parents' own relationship with computers and their perception of their children's relationship with computers. Parent responses to the questions were videotaped, transcribed, and analyzed. When reviewing the data that surfaced it was noted that three parent interview questions in particular focused on the importance of computer knowledge, access to computers, and adults guiding children's development of computer knowledge. Interview Question 16 addresses the issue of computer knowledge: Do you think young children need to learn about how to use computers? Through the collection and analysis of parent interview responses a view emerged for what participant parents consider the significance of computers in their children's lives.

The parents interviewed all offered affirmative responses which agreed with the perspective that their children definitely need to learn about how to use computers. Four of the six parents or 66% of the parents responded with the exact word "Absolutely" and 33% of parents interviewed offered a response of "Yes." The words chosen to respond to Question 16 demonstrate strong parental views concerning the question of children needing to know how to use computers. Parental rationales for why their children need to know how to use computers related to their children's educational endeavors, as well as future employment opportunities, and the impact of computers for every aspect of their children's daily lives.

In her response to Question 16, Elizabeth, the parent of Family 2, presented her view of computer knowledge as a skill that is required in day-to-day life. Elizabeth stated, "It just helps, it makes life easier and it's lots of fun and it's great." This is a positive perspective and the significance of computers in her own life reflects her view: "I use the computer for school, I use the computer to communicate with people, I use the computer for recipes, I mean, just everything." Elizabeth's desire to enable her child to be able to use computers is demonstrated by allowing her young daughter to use the newer home computer with supervision. Victoria does not have to use the nine-year-old computer that Elizabeth said is "not used for much more than being able to color or play some video games."

According to Elizabeth the need for young children to learn to use computers was an enthusiastic "Oh, absolutely. Absolutely." She discussed the challenge and necessity for keeping pace with technology. "Technology is just constantly (changing), if you don't keep up you fall behind. . . they (children) have to keep up and it's in every job basically . . . the computer makes every job easier." This participant parent considers computer knowledge as a skill her daughter needs now and for future employment possibilities. Each parent conveyed a similar perspective in response to the question which focused on the need for young children to learn how to use computers. The perspective of these study parents is that computer knowledge is a skill that young children need to acquire.

Common Goals for Acquiring Computer Knowledge

The third question of this study utilized parent interviews and study data to scrutinize common goals of participant parents for their 6-year-old children's acquisition of computer knowledge. The collection of data which focused on the third research question included six videotaped parent interviews, videotaped site visits, researcher observations, and field notes. The resulting videotapes were transcribed and analyzed, with field notes examined. The resulting analysis uncovered common goals for acquisition of computer knowledge that participant parents want for their children.

The first common goal that the researcher considers to be revealed from the collection, analysis, and interpretation of data is that the parents interviewed all appear to have the common perspective that their children need to be able to know how to use a computer. Parent interview responses confirm that being able to use a computer will impact academic success as well as future employment opportunities. During her parent interview Aileen, the Family 5 mother, said, "Soon he's going to start doing homework on the computer." Barbara, the mother in Family 6, shared her view as, "When you (students) get in older grades rather than pick up a dictionary or an encyclopedia you can go on to the Internet to do your research." According to Family 4 mother Gina, "When they (children) get in the working world . . . everything is computerized. Everything." Patrick Sr. of Family 1 stated, "Everything these days is somehow computer based." These parents consider computers and technology as part of everyday life in the society in which their children live.

Common Goal of Opportunities to Interact with Computers

Data were obtained by the researcher during parent interviews which presented the range of opportunities that the parents were able to offer their 6-year-old children with regard to home interaction with computers. The participant families in this study all have computers in their homes and have enabled their children to have computer access from a young age. For all parents interviewed a common goal for acquiring computer knowledge seems to be to offer their children opportunities to interact with computers. During interviews all participant parents discussed how their 6-year-old children were 2 or 3 years old when they first started to interact with computers. Therefore, these 6-year-old children have already been exposed to computers for 3 or 4 years. The common goal of offering their children an opportunity to interact with computers has been achieved by having a working home computer available for use.

When children use more than one computer the knowledge gained from the home computer can be used to understand how to use other computers. At times, all the study children had access to computers in the school setting. Participant parents offered their children access to computers outside the home setting. Whether the location was the library or an after-school program, the children had opportunities outside of the home setting to use computers. A common goal for participant study parents was to offer their children access to computers in a variety of locations.

Common Goal of Increasing Computer Knowledge

The videotaped and transcribed parent interviews and home site visits along with written and reviewed field notes enabled the researcher to collect, analyze, and interpret parental perspectives concerning their 6-year-old children learning how to use computers. A common goal for participant parents seemed to be to increase their children's knowledge of how to use computers. Each participant parent offered their children an opportunity to interact with computers by having a home computer available and allowing time to interact with the computer. Each participant parent interviewed discussed how their child's knowledge of how to turn the computer on or use software programs has grown since their child's introduction to computers and over the past few years. Participant parents having a home computer, allowing time for their children to interact with the computer, and offering guidance as their children interact with a home computer demonstrate how these parents are attempting to achieve this goal of their 6-year-old children increasing their computer knowledge.

Common Goal of Independent Computer Interaction

The analysis and interpretation of data revealed information about the independent computer interaction of the 6-year-old participant children. The researcher contemplated another common computer-related goal for the participant parents, which was that participant parents want their 6-year-old children to be able to interact with a computer independently. The researcher noted that for each participant parent and on repeated occasions, parents would offer guidance or encouragement to their 6-year-old child and then suspend the assistance. At times a parent would make a comment, physically remove themselves from proximity to their child at the computer, or silently watch and not talk while the child continued to interact with the computer. An example of a participant parent encouraging their child's independent computer action is when Patrick Sr. was sitting next to Patrick Jr. and was guiding him with a software program on the computer. The child was trying to decide how to proceed with the game. Patrick Jr. asked a question about how he should proceed and his father said, "You tell me, I'm not telling you." A few seconds later as the child proceeded with continuing to interact with the software program Patrick Sr. said, "I'm not telling you. You do. You pick. Good choice."

Kyle's mother would leave the area but verbally confirmed with her child to let her know if he needed assistance, "Okay, I'm going upstairs; if you need anything, shout." Kyle called his mother if there was a computer glitch but otherwise he would independently interact with the computer. Patrick Jr.'s mother sat behind him as he operated the hardware or software of the computer. Christina, Patrick Jr.'s mother, would watch as he interacted with the computer and would offer brief responses that did not guide the child's actions. Some of her comments were "really," "probably," "maybe," or "you never know" in response to some of Patrick Jr.'s questions during interaction with computer software or an Internet web site.

All six children would, at times, work independently at their home computers. Levels of proficiency varied but all of the children in this study independently interacted and utilized a computer. Common goals by participant parents for their children's acquisition of computer knowledge included offering opportunities for their children to interact with computers at home and outside the home, encouraging their children to increase knowledge attained about computers, and being able to independently interact with computers. The parents interviewed viewed attainment of these goals as offering educational and occupational opportunities for their children.

Summary of Findings for Research Question Three

Parent interview responses indicated parental perspectives for the significance of computers in their children's lives. Computers are important for their children to succeed educationally, for future employment, and to function in everyday life. These six parents want their children to be able to function and participate in the technological world the children are growing up in. Computers are seen as a tool that is part of everyday life at home, in the library, and at school. The significance of computers in the lives of their children is as a tool and a link. Computers can be used as a tool to make life easier, such as looking up a word online instead of in a book. These parents view computers as an essential element in the lives of their children, and as a link for future employment and career opportunities. Participant parents viewed computers as allowing their children to succeed now and in future endeavors. Computers are viewed as being linked to educational and employment opportunities. Parents in the current study had goals for their 6-year-old children relating to learning how to use computers, expanding their knowledge of how to use computers, and being able to independently interact with computers. Access to computers was offered by participant parents for their 6-year-old children in the home setting and community settings such as the library.

Parents in the study demonstrated through their actions that they consider computers important in the lives of their young children. All six families have a computer in the home, participant parents guide their 6-year-old children as interaction with a home computer occurs, and participant parents offer their young children access to computers outside the home setting. Observations of the six families studied using a case study approach offered qualitative data that permitted examination of the third research question.

SUMMARY OF STUDY FINDINGS

In this section a summary of the study is offered which includes the problem, procedure, instruments, research setting, data analysis, and findings. A review of the research questions and resulting findings is presented. The implications for adults guiding young children developing an understanding of how to use computers are considered, and a discussion of further research needed is presented.

The Problem

From school to work, and even shopping, computers are an integral part of daily life in American society (Wartella & Jennings, 2000). Currently parental perceptions of computers are positive with over 90% of parents viewing the computer as important for their child's education and future opportunities (Land, 1999). The view of skills such as literacy gradually emerging in young children is a perspective which may be applied to the acquisition of computer knowledge (Ba, Tally, & Tsikalas, 2002).

There is a critical need for research to explore computer knowledge as the skill develops while young children and their parents interact with computers in the home setting. Parents being observed while guiding their young children's interaction with home computers may offer an understanding of approaches adults may use to guide children at computers. The resulting awareness of how parents offer guidance and access to computers for young children in the home setting may offer implications for teachers using computers with children in the school setting.

Research Questions

Through the review of the data collected and analyzed, information surfaced to be able to respond to the three research questions:

1. What strategies do these parents utilize to offer their children guidance and access to computers?
2. What language categories and patterns do these parents utilize to guide their young children interacting with computers?
3. What do these parents consider the significance of computers in their children's lives and what are common goals for their children's acquisition of computer knowledge?

Procedure

The research procedure which was adhered to in the current study was to: (a) obtain authorization from proper authorities to conduct current research; (b) contact and recruit participant families; (c) obtain permission to conduct observations; (d) conduct six parent interviews; (e) conduct four site visits for each of the six families; (f) analyze data; (g) discuss findings; (h) offer recommendations for further research.

Instruments

Parent Computer Perspective Interview

A germane tool used for the study was the Parent Computer Perspective Interview questionnaire. To understand parent views about computers, their own use of computers, and the use of computers by their children, parents were asked 20 questions. The categories for questions were: (a) general information; (b) household computer information; (c) parent's computer information and use; (d) child's computer information and use; (e) family computer information and use; and (f) parent attitudes about computers. Verbal instructions were read to parents before interviews began. The choice of a long interview questionnaire format permitted the researcher to ask questions in the same order while allowing an opportunity for follow-up questions (McCracken, 1988). The results attained by using the long interview format to question parents enabled inferences to be drawn from adult participants in the study.

Adult Language Categories

The tool that was developed for the current study was the Mele Robinson Content Analysis Coding Sheet (see Appendix D). This instrument allowed transference of videotapes into transcriptions to be able to dissect verbal and nonverbal parent and child computer activity. Adult language and parent-child discourse were analyzed using the coding sheet. The types of language categories parents used while talking to their children emerged from parent-child talk observed during the pilot study. The adult word phrases were grouped as conversational language, inquiry language, directive language, validating language, or procedural language. Was the parent talking to the child, was a question asked, was the child directed to complete an action, did the adult explain the function of computer hardware or software, or did the adult encourage the child verbally for actions taken?

From the transcriptions, the frequency of parent language was able to be sorted according to the five adult language categories, with totals obtained for each family and for each site visit. The resulting frequency count permitted language category totals, percentages, and commonalities to emerge. The information that resulted from the adult language categories assisted in gaining an understanding of how these parents guided their children with computers.

Parent-Child Discourse Coding

Talk between parents and their children was also coded with the Mele Robinson Content Analysis Coding Sheet by the type of discourse that transpired. Discourse coding consisted of analysis of talk between parents and their children at the computer. Was the talk a discussion, was a question being asked, was the talk a response to a question, or was a parent offering a child feedback for a statement made? The frequency of incidences of discussion, inquiry, response, and feedback of mother, father, or child were tallied and then totaled. The nonverbal actions occurring were used to corroborate verbal information and outcomes within and across parents and children. The resulting frequency count permitted discourse coding totals, percentages, and commonalities to surface. The information that resulted from coding parent-child discourse was vital in forming an understanding of how these parents guided their children during computer activity time.

Research Setting

Participants

There were eight parents and their 6-year-old children participating in the current study. The families live in homes located in Staten Island, New York. The study focused on parents guiding their children at a home computer with six mothers, two fathers, and six children participating in the study. Additional family members were in the home setting during site visits but the above mentioned participants are the individuals being considered for the study.

As in the feasibility study the 6-year-old children were students currently attending public schools in Staten Island, New York. All of the children were 6 years of age. Three of the children participating in the study were male and three were female. There was one single-parent family and the other five families were dual-parent households. None of the children were eligible for the free lunch program at their schools. During the researcher's prearranged visits to participant homes, six mothers guided their 6-year-old children at the computer 92% of the time. Of the five study family fathers, only two were home and available to offer guidance 8% of the time. A focal point of the study was home visit observations of mothers and fathers offering guidance to their 6-year-old children during computer interaction.

Parent Interview Protocol

One parent from each of the participating families was interviewed using the 20 questions from the Parent Computer Perspective Interview (see Appendix B). Each session began with the researcher placing the video camera on a tripod and directing the camera toward the parent. The record button was pressed and then the researcher would begin reading the interview directions. The 20 questions were read in sequential order with the researcher responding to any clarifying questions parents asked about an interview question. Follow-up questions were asked by the researcher when a parent's response was brief or did not seem to respond to the question being asked. Additional dialogue would occur if a parent's response prompted additional questions or discussion. After the parent interview was completed the video camera record button was pressed again to stop camera recording. Upon completion of the parent interview, the researcher confirmed the date and time for the first site visit for computer observations.

Site Visit Protocol

Visits to the homes of participating families were arranged by the researcher with parents and conducted in the daytime, evening, during the week, or on the weekend at agreed upon dates and times. The researcher would arrive, greet family members, and place the video camera on a tripod for recording. The camera was placed behind and to the side of where the computer was located. As soon as the camera was set up on the tripod, the record button was pressed to record activity at the computer. The researcher sat next to the camera and observed activity occurring at the computer while taking field notes. The site visit would end and video recording would stop when the child concluded computer interaction.

Data Analysis

During the study data were collected from a variety of sources including parent interview videotapes, site visit notes, and site visit videotapes. Data were analyzed using both qualitative and quantitative methods. Upon completion of data collection, videotapes were transcribed in preparation for analysis. The descriptive qualitative analysis that resulted was derived from review of the researcher's computer activity sheet field notes, as well as videotapes and transcriptions. Quantitative analysis resulted from frequency counts of parent language categories and parent-child discourse with the end result being the emergence of frequency count totals, percentages, and commonalities among parents. Assessment of qualitative and quantitative data permitted conclusions to be obtained concerning the approaches parents use to guide their children with computers and access to computers that parents offer their children.

Findings

A case study approach for this research study permitted the naturalistic observation of parents guiding and offering access to their young children using computers. The use of observation in the home setting replicates the research setting utilized by researchers examining emergent literacy in young children (Dickinson & Tabors, 2001; Storch & Whitehurst, 2001; Teale, 1986). Triangulation of data was obtained by the use of videotapes, field notes, and transcriptions. The resulting findings were the foundation for responding to the three research questions of the study.

Research Question One

Videotapes, field notes, as well as transcriptions from parent interviews and site observations were the basis for responding to research question one: What strategies do these parents utilize to offer their children guidance and access to computers? Parents in this study used various strategies to offer their children guidance with a home computer. During site visits the researcher observed and a video camera recorded parents in close proximity to their children when offering one-on-one guidance at the computer. These children were consistently offered a response when they verbally requested assistance with the home computer. All parent reactions consisted of a verbal response and then action. Some of the parents were already near the computer and others moved within closer proximity when called but all parents reacted and offered their children guidance.

For the question of access to computers the resulting information was that the six families all had a computer in the home setting. Owning a home computer was a criterion for participation in the current study and a commonality to all families. These parents had offered their children access to a home computer from the age of 2 or 3. For five of the six children initial exposure to computers occurred in the home setting.

Participant parents offered their children access to computers and did not limit computer time as a way to reprimand their children. These children were also offered access to computers in locations outside of the home setting including libraries and after-school computer classes. Strategies used by these parents to offer their children guidance and access to computers were to consistently respond when assistance was needed, to be in close proximity when offering assistance, to refrain from limiting computer time as a form of behavioral reprimand, and to offer access in different arenas. The perspective of these parents was that computers are an educational tool that these children need to succeed in school and for future career opportunities.

Research Question Two

Videotapes, transcriptions, and field notes offered information that was analyzed and used to respond to research question two: What language categories and patterns do these parents utilize to guide their young children interacting with computers? Using transcriptions, adult language categories were decided for the parent talking with their child at the computer. The language categories were inquiry language, conversational language, directive language, procedural language, and validating language. Frequency counts for each category were tallied and totaled for each and all site visits. Resulting percentages were calculated for each parent, for each site visit, for all site visits, and for comparison across parents. Language was one of the tools these parents used for guiding their children at the computer. The predominant adult language category was conversational language with computer-related talk. The pattern of parents coming within close proximity when their child called and verbally requested assistance was a commonality for all parents.

The talk occurring between parents and their children was coded from the transcriptions using the discourse coding categories of mother inquiry, father inquiry, child inquiry, mother response, father response, child response, mother discussion, father discussion, child discussion, mother feedback, and father feedback. After the frequency counts were totaled the categories of mother and father were combined into one category for parent inquiry, parent response, and parent feedback. Frequency counts were converted into percentages for discourse categories. The discourse category occurring most often was discussion which consisted of parent discussion (31%) and child discussion (30%).

Parents in Families 1, 2, and 3 were in the area where their children were interacting with computers. For Families 1 and 3 the two top rank order discourse categories were parent discussion and child discussion. For Family 2 the two top rank order discourse categories were child discussion and parent discussion. The remaining five items were in the same rank order for all three families: PI-CI-CR-PR-PF. The rank order of discourse categories for these three families may be due to the proximity of parents which enabled adult guidance to be possible or due to chance. Further research would be needed to reveal the reason for the patterns that emerged and the significance to the quality of a child's computer experience.

Research Question Three

Parent interview responses that were videotaped and transcribed in preparation for analysis, along with researcher field notes from observations, were used to be able to examine research question three: What do these parents consider the significance of computers in their children's lives and what are common goals for their children's acquisition of computer knowledge? These parents consider computers as important for success in school and for careers later in life. All of the parents interviewed agreed that young children do need to learn how to use computers. Four of the parents actually chose the word "absolutely" to convey their level of enthusiasm for children needing to learn about how to use computers. Parents' actions confirm their perspective about the importance of computers as these parents guided their children with computers and offered computer access outside the home setting at libraries or with after-school computer classes.

A common goal that these parents have for their children's acquisition of computer knowledge was that these parents want their children to increase their knowledge of how to use computers. These parents have offered their children opportunities to experiment and explore with a home computer. Through assistance and guidance from their parents, these children are learning how to construct and develop knowledge of how to use a computer.

Another goal that was common to all families is that these parents want their children to be able to independently interact with computers. This was demonstrated as parents offered their children guidance at the computer and then encouraged their child to also independently interact without adult intervention. During the 24 site visits, the six children often requested assistance from their parents to resolve computer glitches, challenges, and problems with software and hardware. Parents would offer computer assistance and then encourage their child to continue to independently interact with the computer hardware or software. Acquisition of computer knowledge is a journey and a goal for these parents guiding their children at home computers.

Talk at the Computer

In this study discourse occurring at the computer was analyzed using Mele Robinson's Content Analysis Coding Sheet. The format of Inquiry-Response-Discussion-Feedback (IqDRF) is one way to scrutinize talk at the computer. Cazden (2001) explored traditional lessons in the school setting with the discourse analysis format of Initiation (I), Response (R), and Feedback (F). Cazden also examined talk at the computer using the format of Initiation (I), Discussion (D), Response (R), and Follow-up (F) or IDRF.

In this study the discourse analysis format of IqDRF was employed with discussion (D) being the highest parent-child combined discourse category at 61%. Inquiry was the second highest combined parent-child discourse category with 25% of the talk during time at the computer (see Figure 4.17). In the home setting the traditional school discourse format of IDRF did not seem to be relevant. Discussion with 31% of parent talk and 30% of child talk was the dominant discourse category. Parent-child discussion at the computer was part of the dynamic which allowed these six children to be able to be engaged and sustain interaction with their home computers. The resulting use of discussion and inquiry discourse for adults guiding children with computers could be considered for use in the school setting. Teachers could use discussion and inquiry as tools when guiding young children interacting with computers. This possible strategy would need further research to discover if the suggested implication could have a positive impact in educational settings.

STUDY CONCLUSION

A case study approach was utilized for this study which considered the ways parents of six families guided their 6-year-old children with home computers. The use of a video camera, anecdotal notes, and resulting transcriptions offered a triangulation of information that was able to be analyzed. The subsequent data resulted in frequency counts, percentages, and patterns.

In conclusion, the current study is a beginning step toward understanding how parents are able to guide young children in understanding how to use computers. The relevance of an adult in close proximity to talk with and guide a child's experience at the computer was noted in the current study. An adult using conversational language to discuss computer-related topics with a child was considered an applicable approach for guiding children at computers. An adult asking questions, when they were not-in-close proximity or were unclear about the child's computer challenge, allowed the adult to clarify what the child was doing on the computer. The strategies that participant parents used to guide their young children in the home setting can be considered as possibilities for use by educators in a school setting. Further research on the topic of adults offering children access to computers and supporting emerging computer knowledge is needed to understand how to guide young children.

5   Research Implications

IMPLICATIONS FOR ADULTS GUIDING YOUNG CHILDREN

The current research adopted a case study approach of observing what happened in the home setting as young children interacted with computers and parents offered guidance. There were six families in the study which is a limited group for offering generalizations. Nonetheless, the lessons learned from this research study of parents interacting with their children at home computers offer implications for computer use in home and school settings. Adult strategies that can be learned from the current study are for teachers to be in close proximity to children working at computers, for an adult to engage in discourse with a child using a computer, and for an educator to consistently provide assistance when a student requests computer help.

Emergence of Computer Knowledge in Young Children

The term computer literacy has changed numerous times since being coined by Arthur Luehrmann in 1972 (Moursund, 2003). A current agreed upon definition of computer literacy does not exist. How can parents or teachers seek to achieve a goal of assisting children to become computer literate if a clear definition of the term does not exist? A single definition of the term computer literacy is needed to allow parents, educators, and researchers to comprehend the goal children are being guided toward.

The definition of computer literacy that is utilized for the current research is proposed by the organization CL-USA (2007). According to CL-USA (2007) that definition is:

> An understanding of the concepts, terminology and operations that relate to general computer use. It is the essential knowledge needed to function independently with a computer. This functionality includes the ability to solve and avoid problems, adapt to new situations, keep information organized and communicate effectively with other computer literate people. (p. 1)

The current study confirms the use of an "emergent skills" approach when trying to understand how young children develop computer knowledge. By understanding emergent literacy and the relationship to computer knowledge, a perspective is given that frames the strategies that have been discussed of how parents support children's growing understanding of how to use computers. In 1966 Marie Clay offered the term "emergent literacy" to describe the behaviors she observed in young children when interacting with books and writing materials that eventually developed into conventional literacy skills. The acquisition of literacy was viewed as "an active, constructive process" (Christie, Enz, & Vukelich, 2003, p. 118). In the emergent view of literacy, the journey to becoming literate begins in infancy when being read to, during early attempts to write, through exploration and experimentation as a child grows, and by support of prominent adults in a child's environment (Christie et al., 2003; Clay, 1966; Soderman, Gregory, & O'Neill, 1999).

Literacies are considered as always being emergent and as being situated within particular practices and communities. As presented in the Center for Children and Technology Report (Behrman, 2000) literacy is considered an emergent process whether the literacy is traditional reading and writing or emergent computer skills. The emergent literacy concept of skills growing through a child's exposure to environmental materials with opportunities to explore and experiment, guided by significant adults in the environment, is an analogy for understanding a child's development of computer literacy (Ba et al., 2002).

Emergent literacy skills are supported and guided in the home setting by parents (Dickinson & Tabors, 2001; Storch & Whitehurst, 2001; Sulzby & Teale, 1996; Teale, 1986). Who introduces children to computers, as well as when and where, are topics to be considered when trying to comprehend how children develop an understanding of how to use computers. Parents are able to offer their children exposure to, access to, and guidance with computers in the home setting as computer knowledge develops and computer literacy skills emerge. The perspective of computer knowledge being an emergent skill offers educational implications for teachers guiding young children with computers in school settings and is supported by the current research.

Close Proximity

The first inference for adults guiding children with computers is that when children are interacting with computers, an adult being in close proximity to assist enables a child to continue to be engaged with computer activity. The current research validates what might seem to some educators to be an obvious statement. When an adult is in close proximity to a child during computer activity, the adult is aware of what the child is doing. The adult is able to observe if the child is capable of successful interaction with a computer's hardware and software, or if assistance or guidance is needed. As an adult reads the computer screen or discusses the activity with the child, the adult is ready and able to offer timely guidance when the child needs assistance. The child does not have to call an adult to the computer to assist or explain what the difficulty is. An adult being close by allows the child to discuss the activity and be more likely to be continuously engaged with computer interaction.

As an observer in elementary school classrooms for over 10 years, the author has observed kindergarten children working independently at computers that were set up with software programs ready to be used by children while teachers conducted other activities with the rest of the class. If the children needed assistance with computer problems or did not understand how to interact with the game, interrupting the teacher to ask was not an option many children chose. Therefore, by not having an adult in close proximity, computer time often was a frustrating and unproductive time for many of these children. If a teacher offers children access and time to use computers when available to be nearby for questions or to help resolve challenges, the teacher is aware of the children's actions. The teacher would be aware of what computer activities the children are interacting with and could scaffold computer activity time to enable the children to remain engaged with the computer.

Importance of Talk at the Computer

The second inference for adults guiding children with computers is the importance of talk at the computer. When an adult is in close proximity to a child, talk, having a discussion, or asking questions about what is occurring with a software program, web site activity, or computer hardware is possible. For Family 1 and Family 3 in the current study, parents in close proximity allowed their children to try different software programs or web sites, in addition to children being assisted when using software programs, web sites, or computer's hardware. Parents were able to discuss computer activity choices or ask their children about actions taken. The discussion and guidance of these parents allowed their children to have sustained successful interaction with novel computer information. If these parents were not engaged in talk while in close proximity then this guided exploration could not have occurred. The quality of a child's computer experience is at times able to be enhanced by adult involvement. Talk between adult and child is a positive asset to the child's learning experience.

In the school setting, talk at the computer might occur among children using a computer together or between a child and a teacher as children use classroom computers. By having a conversation with children interacting with computer hardware, software, or an online site, a teacher can use questioning strategies that are also used during class time. As observed in the study, talk at the computer was predominantly focused *on the computer.* Through discussion and questioning, a teacher can offer questions that provoke critical thinking skills in the young computer users.

Access to Computers

Another implication that was noted from the study is that an adult is able to offer a child access to computers in different locations with different computers. This variation in access locations enables a child to use different computers outside the home setting. The experience of using alternate computers, rather than only the home computer, enables the specific knowledge gained to be generalized. Familiarity with using different computers builds on a child's computer knowledge and ability to apply understandings acquired from use of a home computer.

As of 2003, 84.5% of American schoolchildren from kindergarten through 12th grade were using computers in school, with 72.2% of children between the ages of 5 and 7 given computer access (United States Census, 2003). Having access to computers in the school setting is beneficial, in particular for children who do not have a computer available at home. Teachers may offer opportunities in the school setting for a child to use computers and also to use different computers. There may be computers in the classroom, the school library, the local library, or in other settings. There might be desktop computers, laptop computers, or tablet computers on hand. There might be Dell, Gateway, or Apple computer brands present for the children to use. Having access to various computers in different settings allows children to learn to interact not only with a specific computer but with different equipment and programs. Encouraging children to gain access to different brands or types of computers will provide them with opportunities to experiment and explore, as well as build skills and knowledge about how to use computers.

Independent Computer Time

In the current study 65% of the children had opportunities some time during the site visits to independently interact with their home computer. During independent activity time the children chose software games available on their computer or visited parent-approved Internet sites. Independent activity time allowed the children to test knowledge gained and try to expand on what had previously been learned. Children who are provided opportunities to independently interact with computers have the possibility of experimenting and exploring with a computer's software and hardware.

In an educational setting when computer time is assigned in a Computer Laboratory, students often have to complete the activities scripted by the instructor. Allowing a child the opportunity for discovery during independent computer activity time enables the child to problem solve creatively and gain understandings that might not be achieved through direct instruction. Just as children learn to play an instrument by experimenting with the sound of notes, or begin to master reading by sitting with a book and figuring out the meanings of the words, the same independent adventures are needed when gaining an understanding of how to use a computer.

Digital Natives and Digital Immigrants

When thinking about children using computers in the home setting and then deliberating the implications of computers in the school setting, the issue of young children who are now growing up with and being surrounded ubiquitously with computers needs to be considered. Marc Prensky (2001a) coined the terms "digital natives" and "digital immigrants" to offer analogies for the generation gap between computer users (p. 1). The nuances of young children growing up with computers, who are digital natives, differ from adults who have had to learn about computers later in life and are considered digital immigrants (Facer et al., 2003, p. 3).

According to Prensky (2001a) "Our students have changed radically. Today's students are no longer the people our educational system was designed to teach" (p. 1). Teachers who are digital immigrants struggle at times to teach a student population that speaks a totally different digital language. As seen in Table 5.1, Jukes and Dosaj (2003) present an interesting comparison of digital native students and their digital immigrant teachers. There are problems that are caused by the differences between how digital native students learn and how digital immigrant teachers teach. The current school system was designed for an agrarian and manufacturing world so it is easy to understand the resulting disconnect between how students learn and how teachers teach (Jukes & Dosaj, 2003).

Through discussions with college students, the researcher has noted that when adults, who are now teachers, were taught to read, they were taught to look at the text first and then to look at the illustration that accompanied a story. Today, the author has observed that when young children read, they often look at the visual images first and then at the words of the story. Teachers are not always able to use the same strategies they were taught when instructing young children who are growing up in a different world. The digital immigrants and digital natives are from two different *cultures*. Should the digital immigrant teachers fully adapt their teaching strategies to their digital native students? Should the digital native students accommodate their immigrant teachers and lose their technological perspective when in the school setting? This researcher agrees with VanSlyke (2003) that "Cultural assimilation rarely entails a wholesale abandonment of previous customs or practices; rather, it

Table 5.1 The Differences Between Digital Native Learners and Digital Immigrant Teachers

Digital Native Learners	Digital Immigrant Teachers
Prefer receiving information quickly from multiple multimedia sources.	Prefer slow and controlled release of information from limited sources.
Prefer parallel processing and multitasking.	Prefer singular processing and single or limited tasking.
Prefer processing pictures, sounds and video before text.	Prefer to provide text before pictures, sounds and video.
Prefer random access to hyperlinked multimedia information.	Prefer to provide information linearly, logically and sequentially.
Prefer to interact/network simultaneously with many others.	Prefer students to work independently rather than network and interact.
Prefer to learn "just-in-time."	Prefer to teach "just-in-case" (it's on the exam).
Prefer instant gratification and instant rewards.	Prefer deferred gratification and deferred rewards.
Prefer learning that is relevant, instantly useful and fun.	Prefer to teach to the curriculum guide and standardized tests.

*Ian Jukes and Anita Dosaj, The InfoSavvy Group, February 2003

typically involves a flexible process of negotiation and adaptation, wherein certain elements of both cultures are retained in a new combination with one another" (¶ 14). Teachers, who did not have computers as part of their world during childhood, need to be prepared to offer guidance with computers to children who are comfortable in the new digital world.

The current research did not focus on the issue of digital immigrants and digital natives but the two dynamics can be contemplated for the adults and children in the study. During the parent interviews, all of the adults discussed how they did not grow up with computers as part of their daily lives. Therefore, the adults in the current study are considered digital immigrants. The 6-year-old children in the study had technology as part of their daily lives since the age of 2 or 3. Thus, the children are considered to be digital natives. Despite being digital immigrants, these parents have successfully guided these digital natives in developing an understanding of how to use computers.

The resulting implication in this study for digital immigrants being able to guide digital natives is that these parents did not have to be computer experts to be able to guide their children with computers. Although these parents could not always resolve the computer hardware and software glitches that were encountered, the adult involvement in the learning process allowed the children to continue to be engaged with the computer. The children's computer activity choices might have been altered but the children did not have to cease computer interaction due to dilemmas encountered. These digital immigrant parents were able to effectively guide their digital native children to problem solve computer challenges by selecting an alternative computer activity. The implication of this realization for the school setting is that teachers do not need to be computer experts or digital natives to guide the young children in their classes. In order to be able to guide young children with computers an educator does need to possess basic computer skills. The adult would need to understand how to turn a computer on, how to access software programs, and how to redirect a young child's activity choice when computer problems do occur. With basic computer knowledge, digital immigrant adults are still able to offer guidance and problem-solving options for digital natives to enable young children to remain engaged with computer activities.

In 2002, 92% of American schoolchildren had Internet connectivity in their schools (Evans, 2007). These students who were in sixth grade at that time will be freshmen in college in 2014. By the year 2018 and beyond, college students that were exposed to computers at a young age in the school setting will be graduating and may become teachers. Therefore, in approximately 10 years adults who are digital natives will be teaching children who are also digital natives. In the interim teachers do not need to be overwhelmed by the thought of guiding children with computers. The availability of an adult to give directions, suggestions, and alternate paths of action allows a child to observe problem-solving skills that are needed to effectively maneuver computers.

COMPUTER LITERACY DEVELOPMENT

In the current research the acquisition of computer literacy is viewed from a developmental contextual perspective as being analogous to literacy skills. Therefore, just as literacy learning begins early and is an ongoing process, computer literacy skills are also being proposed from an emergent skills perspective. "Readers and writers go through three stages of development: emergent literacy, early literacy, and independent literacy" (Slegers, 1996, p. 4). Literacy skills of reading and writing emerge over time and the possibility is being presented that computer knowledge materializes gradually. The three stages of Computer Literacy Development (CLD) being proposed by Mele Robinson are Emergent Computer Literacy, Early Computer Literacy, and Independent Computer Literacy. The stages of literacy development are being utilized as a framework for understanding the emergence of computer literacy.

For researchers attempting examination of the concept of computer literacy, collective agreement for a definition of the term is essential but not available at this time. The lack of an agreed upon definition of the term computer literacy has existed since the 1970s when computers began to develop as part of the educational landscape. A shared consensus for the definition of the term would provide a framework for scholarly exploration of the topic.

Educators and researchers have been developing an understanding of computer literacy and the stages adults go through when learning about computers (King, 2002). An integrated computer literacy perspective would consider computers as part of an individual's lifelong learning experience. The phases within each stage consider which elements of computer knowledge a computer user is trying to grasp and acquire. A developmental perspective is being offered as a starting point for discussion of how knowledge of using computers might surface and develop in learners.

Children's Initial Use of Computers

What is being presented with the CLD stages is the concept that the skills needed to successfully interact with computers are acquired and develop gradually. The CLD perspective for the acquisition of computer knowledge is that the process of learning about computers begins when a child is very young and an understanding continues to grow and develop as a child matures. The issue of an individual who has not been exposed to computers until an older age is discussed in the Independent Computer Literacy phase. For a young child between the ages of 1 and 2, the process of developing an understanding of computers begins with the initial awareness of the machine called a *computer* being present. When a computer is part of a child's primary care setting, a 1- or 2-year-old child might be aware of an adult, child, or possibly family members sitting at this machine and being engaged in activities.

A computer is another device in the home or primary care setting, just as a television or telephone is a tool being operated by individuals in the setting. Over time the child may become aware of adults, children, or family members interacting with a computer. As with other learning situations, a young child might want to emulate what family members have been observed doing. An awareness of the tool and a desire to interact with a computer is the beginning of a lifelong learning process.

There are two environments to consider when contemplating initiation with computers: the primary care setting and the educational setting. A primary care setting might be the child's home environment, a family day-care setting, or a babysitter's home. An educational setting could be the child's nursery school, after-school program, local library, or community center. In the primary care setting the child may be offered individual computer use. In an educational setting computer activity time may involve a small group of two, three, or four children all working on one computer at the same time. The environment will determine the approach that should be utilized for initiation of computers with young children.

The NAEYC (1996) Technology Position Statement advocates a child being at least 3 years of age for initiation with computers. In a group setting such as school, this researcher agrees that age 3 works well for the introduction of computers. As an early childhood director, the author developed a program where the preschool teachers offered computers to children in the 3- and 4-year-old classrooms. In the classroom setting with 2-year-olds where the author worked, the teachers and director agreed that computers would not have been appropriate in this group setting. In the home setting when a young child is able to be guided one-on-one by an adult, the author agrees that a child may begin using a computer at the age of 2 or possibly younger. In this setting an adult is able to guide a young child one-on-one so the computer will be used appropriately.

During the current research study, three of the parents indicated that their child's initial exposure to computers occurred in the home setting when the child was 2 years old. Parents comfortable with technology who have a child showing an interest in interacting with a computer may allow a 2-year-old child to use a home computer. When a child is sitting on an adult's lap, known as laptime, the adult is able to offer the necessary one-on-one guidance to a young child. If a child shows a genuine interest in computer use and is not being pushed by an adult who wants to teach a child, then offering guidance and brief times at the computer can be a positive adult-child activity, whether the adult is a parent or the child's babysitter. The viewpoint being advocated here is for parents to allow their young children access and guidance to use computers when the child is developmentally ready and has the intellectual capacity to do so.

A young child may demonstrate a comfort and interest in computers and technology. Five of the study parents provided initial computer access for their children in the home setting. The possibility being presented is that for children ages 2 and older, a parent should consider a child's interest when deciding when to introduce computer usage. Just as parents support and encourage a child who is interested in playing an instrument or playing a sport, so should parents note when a child wants to interact with a computer and guide the child's learning experience.

Educators and researchers need to remember that many young children are digital natives who are aware of technology tools in the world in which they live. In the future the current provisional learning model being presented would need to be reconsidered to be aligned with the skill levels of future digital natives and how computers will exist within society. A computer is not required in the home setting to offer a child access to computers. There are libraries and other community resources for a parent to give a child access to computers in an educational setting. The choice of whether to offer a 2-year-old child access and opportunity to interact with computers is a parent's choice.

STAGES OF COMPUTER LITERACY DEVELOPMENT

The elements presented in Table 5.2 will be discussed in detail to clarify the emergent approach of computer literacy development. The emergence of computer knowledge being presented is comparable to literacy skills with first Emergent Computer Literacy, next Early Computer Literacy, and finally Independent Computer Literacy. In Emergent Computer Literacy, the elements of computer awareness and learning are considered to be occurring sequentially. In Early Computer Literacy and Independent Computer Literacy the elements within each phase will not adhere to a sequential process. Examination of each phase will clarify the dynamics occurring as a learner develops an understanding of how to use a computer and subsequently acquires computer literacy skills.

Table 5.2 Computer Literacy Development

Emergent Computer Literacy (Age 6 months–2/3 years)

❖ Awareness

❖ Observation

❖ Engagement

❖ Lap Learning

Early Computer Literacy (Age 3/4–7/8 years)

❖ Trial and Error Learning

❖ Directive Learning

❖ Procedural Learning

❖ Experimentation:

      Non-duplicative Actions

      Duplicative Actions

❖ Exploration

Independent Computer Literacy (Age 8/9–Adult)

❖ Continual Early Learning

❖ Knowledge Specific Learning

❖ Menu Based Learning

❖ General Knowledge Learning

❖ Extended Knowledge Learning

❖ Continual Learning

Emergent Computer Literacy

Computer literacy skills emerge over time when a child has a computer as part of their home or school environment. Learning skills begin early and are an ongoing process (Rosberg, 1995) for children. The same process occurs with a child learning to use computers. During Emergent Computer Literacy a very young child is gaining an awareness of computers as part of the primary care setting. The age of the child may be from 6 months through the age of 2 or 3. During this phase the child's awareness of a computer being in the primary care environment may develop into an interest in wanting to interact with a computer. A parent or guardian may choose to offer a child access to computers and enable a child to discover how to interact with a computer. The researcher has noted that there are parents who allow children initiation with computers at 2 or 3 years of age.

Very young children should not be engaging with computers in a formal way during the Emergent Computer Literacy phase. Alternatively, adults or more experienced peers should allow young children interested in interacting with computers opportunities for exploration. Within an emergent literacy framework, children's beginning efforts to interact with computers should be regarded as a legitimate beginning for the acquisition of computer literacy.

Emergent Computer Literacy begins with the Awareness phase, when an infant or very young child may notice that there is a computer in the primary care setting. The child may notice that individuals use the machine that is in the environment. The significance of this phase is that if the important individuals in the primary environment are engaged with the computer, then this tool may be viewed as a desirable one by the child. During this phase the child becomes cognizant of the computer.

Throughout the Observation aspect of Emergent Computer Literacy a child may watch as others in the primary care setting of the home or a childcare provider's home use a computer. A child observing what others are doing when interacting with a computer might have questions and might be trying to understand how to use the tool. The child might be contemplating questions such as: "How do the users get the machine to work? What are the users doing when operating the device? Are they having fun?"

During Engagement a young child will begin to interact with a computer with the help of a parent, guardian, or more experienced peer. Engagement might entail a child being allowed to press a letter on the keyboard, a child pointing to the computer monitor, or being allowed to press the button to turn the computer on or off. The child's engagement with a computer is at the initial point of involvement where the child is offered brief opportunities to interact with the machine.

Eventually a parent, guardian, or more experienced individual might allow a child to go beyond the initial contact with the computer by touching the monitor, mouse, or keyboard and trying to interact with a software program or web site. These activities are often done with the young child sitting on an individual's lap; thus, the Lap Learning phase evolves. Software developers actually employ the term lapware for software programs designed for very young children. During Lap Learning young children are guided by an adult or more experienced peer who permits the child to attempt to interact with a computer.

In Emergent Computer Literacy the child is beginning to become aware of computers in the primary care setting. If given access to computers, awareness progresses to interaction with computers. For a child who demonstrates an interest in learning about computers, adults and experienced peers may enable the initial acquisition of computer literacy skills by offering access to and connection with computers.

Early Computer Literacy

During Early Computer Literacy children are engaged with computer interaction both independently and through the guidance offered from more experienced individuals. Through interaction with computers a child is able to begin to problem solve and figure out how to use a computer. At times the child's solutions occur by chance, such as when randomly clicking on a computer screen using a mouse. At other times the child's action is purposeful, such as using the mouse to click the word start to begin playing a familiar software program. The learning elements occurring during this phase need not be regarded in sequential order. For example, a child may use the Procedural Learning approach to interact independently with a new software program that has a familiar format or be guided by an adult using Directive Learning when understanding how to use a new software program. Early Computer Literacy occurs from the ages of 3 or 4 through the ages of 7 or 8. Children given access to computers from a young age are building their understanding of how to use new and familiar software programs, Internet web sites, and computer equipment.

Trial and Error

During Early Computer Literacy, Trial and Error Learning may occur during a child's independent activity or when being guided by a more experienced adult or peer. A child might attempt to randomly press keys on a computer keyboard in an effort to get a reaction from the software program being used. The child's actions may be successful by chance or might be influenced by the child's previous attempts to use similar computer software or hardware. The computer action of trial and error is a child's unsure act of trying actions to possibly obtain desired results. Trial and Error Learning occurs by chance and may be utilized by a child when a software program is new, a web site is unfamiliar, or the child is unsure of how to use certain computer equipment.

Directive Learning

Next for discussion, but not necessarily in sequential order of occurrence, is Directive Learning. In Directive Learning a child follows the guidance and direction given by a more knowledgeable individual to maneuver the hardware or software of a computer. A child is directed and told what action to take such as "Click on that icon on the screen," or, "Press the enter button on the keyboard." The child follows the directions given but is not offered an explanation for why the actions should be taken. Guidance by a more experienced individual during Directive Learning may enable a child to have sustained computer interaction. A child may be given directions and told what to do while they are interacting with a software program, a web site, or computer hardware. It is interesting to watch young children opt to follow instructions without asking any questions about *why* they are completing the actions. During Directive Learning a child is following orders but not learning about the reasons for the actions. Still, the actions taken during Directive Learning often enable a child to stay engaged when using a computer.

Procedural Learning

When a child is able to independently interact with software programs or computer hardware by adhering to familiar procedures, Procedural Learning is occurring. For example, a child may be familiar with the format offered on the Public Broadcasting Stations (PBS) children's web site http://pbskids.org/. On this site when the cursor is passed over a picture, a voice tells the viewer what the link is. If the cursor is placed on the picture of Big Bird the childlike voice states, "Sesame Street." When the child clicks on Big Bird's picture the action directs the visitor to the Sesame Street web site of games and activities. This same procedure could be used with success by a child interacting with the NOGGIN web site at http://www.noggin.com/index.php?home=1. This site is based on the commercial-free educational channel dedicated to preschoolers. When a child moves the cursor over pictures on the home page, the name of the character and link is stated by an adult male voice.

A child who has used the PBS site could follow procedures used with the PBS site to be able to interact with the NOGGIN web site. Therefore, a child familiar with a certain computer procedure can employ the familiar strategy to successfully engage with the computer program, web site, or computer equipment being utilized. Following familiar procedures might be rewarding when interacting with *some* web sites or programs but using the procedural strategy would not be an appropriate approach for *all* computer challenges encountered.

Experimentation

During Early Computer Literacy while developing computer literacy skills, there is a time of Experimentation. During Experimentation a child may come across an unfamiliar computer challenge such as a new web site or computer game. The child might have to experiment with different computer use strategies to understand how to use the game, tool, or web site. In Experimentation a child attempts purposeful testing of computer hardware, software, or a web site.

When a child is using a new software program, web site, or computer, deciphering how to interact and engage with a novel technology challenge might occur by chance. During a child's chance experimentation the child's actions will at first be non-duplicative and then duplicative. Non-duplicative actions are when a child is initially trying to discover how to use a new piece of hardware or software or even an online web site, and the child cannot explain or duplicate success. For example, by randomly clicking on a computer screen a child might progress from one level to the next when playing a new software program. Through this chance success with clicking on the screen or trying a new maneuver, a child interacting independently with a software program might begin to understand how to play the new computer game. Duplicative actions are when eventually through experimentation and many attempts of interacting with the computer game, the child is able to resolve the software challenge and duplicate the actions taken for a solution.

Duplicative actions during Experimentation occur when a child is able to repeat actions and solve computer challenges purposely. The actions are not completed by chance but are based on previous knowledge obtained. There is a difference between the actions of a child during Trial and Error and the non-duplicative action in use during Experimentation. A child who has prior experience using computers may choose Experimentation as a strategy to try to interact with an unfamiliar computer game, web site, or computer hardware. Even though the action at first cannot be duplicated, the child is consciously trying to utilize prior strategies to understand how to solve the computer challenge being encountered. In this situation the child has some previous encounters with how to independently use a computer's hardware or software and *tries* to figure out how to progress with a game, web site, or computer hardware through experimentation with familiar tactics.

Exploration

Once a child has attained initial success with understanding how to use a computer's software or hardware through experimentation, then exploration can occur to gain additional computer knowledge. Further investigation by the user with somewhat familiar software, hardware, or online ventures encourages the individual to find out what else the program, hardware, or web site is capable of doing. This further investigation is based on knowledge the computer user has about a game, hardware equipment, or online site and is an effort to learn more about the possibilities of interacting with the computer tool on a more advanced level. By exploring the site, software, or equipment further options and additional information are gained to enhance the user's expanding computer knowledge.

Independent Computer Literacy

Independent Computer Literacy occurs at approximately 8 or 9 years of age for a person who has had prior experience with computers. During Independent Computer Literacy the acquisition of computer knowledge would include the ability to use computers or software, as well as engaging in Internet activities. Although the elements of Independent Computer Literacy might not unfold sequentially, each element will be experienced on the journey to gaining computer literacy skills. The development of computer literacy skills are comparative to the development of literacy skills, as "learning is circular or 'recursive'; learners may move forward in some areas and seem to step back as they consolidate understanding in others" (Bank Street College, 2008).

The elements of being computer literate begin to be manifested during the Independent Computer Literacy phase. During Independent Computer Literacy a computer user comes to understand how to interact independently when using computers. This strategy begins during Early Computer Literacy but assistance is often needed for a younger child to remain engaged with using a computer as computer challenges arise. When an individual has a greater storehouse of knowledge and experience, a computer user is more capable of being able to solve and avoid problems, as well as adapt to new situations. By this juncture with using computers, an individual has an understanding of many concepts, terminology, and ways to operate and interact with computers. During Independent Computer Literacy a computer user achieves the knowledge necessary to operate a computer autonomously.

Continual Early Learning

What strategies do computer users select when new computer challenges arise? During Continual Early Learning a computer user will be immersed in the phases that occurred during Early Computer Literacy: Trial and Error, Experimentation, and Exploration. When an individual is new to using computers then selecting the strategies that are available from the Early Computer Literacy phases is occurring for the first time. Computer users, who have had experience with computers from a young age, will choose these familiar strategies of Trial and Error, Experimentation, or Exploration when facing computer challenges. For example Experimentation might be chosen as a strategy to understand an unfamiliar computer format, such as using a tablet computer instead of a desktop.

Knowledge Specific Learning

Another aspect of Independent Computer Literacy is Knowledge Specific Learning, which occurs when an individual is able to interact with a computer or software program because of familiarity with the format or design of a specific brand. During Knowledge Specific Learning a computer user does not know enough about interacting with computers or is not assured enough to generalize the knowledge needed to resolve a computer challenge presented. Therefore if a computer user is familiar with using a Dell computer, then the individual is able to figure out how to use different Dell computers. The knowledge is not able to be generalized if the user needs to interact with a Hewlett-Packard, Gateway, or another brand of computer. During the Knowledge Specific phase a person who knows Dell computers would only understand how to turn a computer on when the power button is in the exact location of Dell computers. In time the individual will understand that pressing a power button, wherever the location is, enables any computer to power up. During the computer learning process there will be a time, even if the time span is brief, during which the learner only has knowledge that is specific to a certain brand format.

Menu Based Learning

During Menu Based Learning of Independent Computer Literacy, an individual is able to engage with a computer software program, computer equipment, or a web site by use of menu bars or toolbars that are familiar to the user. When visiting the home page for the NAEYC web site at http://naeyc. org/ key words for selecting possible topics of interest are listed on the left side of the page. By clicking on key words such as *accreditation, conferences,* or *information for teachers* the user is sent to another page with relevant information about the topic. If the same user was to encounter The Future of Children web site at http://www.futureofchildren.org/index.htm and used the same strategy of selecting and clicking on a key word from the left side of the web page, the same results would occur, and the user would be directed to information about the topic selected. Menu Based Learning is helpful for a learner when attempting to use a new computer program or web site since what the user already knows becomes a resource for problem solving.

The difference between Knowledge Specific Learning and Menu Based Learning is that in Knowledge Specific Learning the user has not gained the ability to generalize. The computer user has not come to understand that different computers can provide similar options. The individual is only able to resolve a computer challenge encountered when the software program or the computer equipment is in the format used by a specific brand format that the user is accustomed to. In Menu Based Learning the user begins to be able to generalize knowledge and would understand that computers, software programs, and web sites have different possible options to choose from in order to obtain the desired resulting action.

General Knowledge Learning

Through the understandings gained during Knowledge Specific Learning and Menu Based Learning, the computer user is able to begin to apply a broad base of computer knowledge that has been gained. During General

Knowledge Learning an individual is able to use the knowledge gained from interaction with specific computers, programs, or web sites. This insight from previous computer experiences enables the user to generalize and attempt to understand how to interact with new or unfamiliar computers, software, or web sites. The base of knowledge that the user possesses permits the individual to be able to interact with computers more independently. The prior computer knowledge base is broad enough for the individual to be able to understand how to negotiate new and unfamiliar computer equipment, new software, or unfamiliar web site formats. During General Knowledge Learning a computer user familiar with one brand of desktop computers would be able to understand how to use another brand of computers. The user might not be able to transfer this knowledge to laptops or tablet computers but can understand different versions of desktop computers. The knowledge gained can be generalized to attempt to engage with unfamiliar hardware, software, or online information.

Extended Knowledge Learning

As learning with computers progresses, the individual will eventually be able to use the cumulative knowledge acquired from computer experiences and be able to successfully interact with novel computer hardware, software programs, or web sites. When this occurs the learner has arrived at Extended Knowledge Learning for the development of computer literacy skills. The learner has gained a vast base of experiences, information, and resources to resolve a wide range of computer challenges that are encountered. For example, if an individual is familiar with desktop computers, using general knowledge gained about computers, the person would be able to comprehend how to operate a tablet computer. The person's base of computer knowledge is able to look at computer challenges and attempt to understand how to solve new issues using previous experiences as the base of knowledge. At this level of computer knowledge the individual is computer literate. As the computer literacy (CL-USA, 2007) definition suggests, a person has the essential knowledge needed to function independently with a computer, has gained an understanding of the concepts, terminology, and operations that relate to general computer use, has the ability to solve and avoid problems, adapt to new situations, keep information organized, and communicate effectively with other computer literate people.

Continual Learning

Finally, during Continual Learning the computer user comes to realize that sustaining computer literacy skills is a continual and collective process with acquisition of computer knowledge being an ongoing endeavor. The computer user understands that there will constantly be new strategies to learn or new tools to grasp. The transformation of storage data devices is one example of a changing computer tool. First, external storage of data files was possible with floppy disks. Then came saving larger amounts of information onto zip drives. Next in the evolution of data storage were CD-ROMs and DVDs. Now there are USB flash drives and Blu-ray Discs for storing larger and larger amounts of data. For a computer literate person in the Continual Learning phase, learning what each new apparatus is and how to use the device is possible. During Continual Learning the individual accepts the reality that in order to maintain computer literacy perpetual acquisition of new computer technology skills is an unending process.

RESEARCH TO PRACTICE

Observing parents guiding their young children in the home setting offered insights into strategies that adults might choose to utilize when scaffolding children's computer experiences in the school setting. Young children given access to computers have a chance to investigate and gain knowledge about how computers work. When an adult is in close proximity and available to assist a child, sustained interaction during computer activity time is feasible. An adult talking at the computer with a child allows for discovery of concepts focused on the computer or encountered through the use of the computer. During interaction with computers young children routinely rely on adults or more knowledgeable peers to provide assistance with computer challenges that surface. At the same time young children also need opportunities for autonomous inquiry to figure out what a computer can and cannot do. The emergence of computer knowledge in young children requires both guided exploration and independent investigation.

The developmental perspective of CLD proposed by Mele Robinson is a provisional hypothesis to prompt a conversation about understanding how young children learn to use computers. As of 2008 there are teachers in early childhood settings who did not grow up being immersed in computers and technology tools day-to-day. Some educators learned about computers in high school or college. By the year 2018 the majority of teachers in the school setting will have had computers as part of their learning throughout their school experience. As the ubiquity of computers increases in the home and school setting, the proposed developmental model would need to be adapted to reflect the changes in learners' emerging computer knowledge. Further computer research in the home and school settings is needed to clarify if the CLD phases, elements, and ages proposed are plausible in comprehending how the acquisition of computer literacy occurs.

6 Supporting Early Computer Literacy Development

How can an early childhood educator guide young children in developing an understanding of how to use computers? One approach is to offer concrete experiences that will assist in developing skills that will be utilized when interacting with computers. This chapter offers hands-on, concrete activities that will build a young child's understanding of how to use computer hardware, software, or Internet sites. Each activity includes an explanation of what the computer skill being taught is, the materials needed to create the activity, and how to play the game. Through the use of these teacher-made, hands-on games young children will be able to gain competencies that will be useful when interacting with computers. Some of the ideas were gleaned from the researchers own experiences working with young children in educational settings with other games being variations from Davidson (1989).

In the 1800s Pestalozzi was the first to assert that young children need to be exposed to concrete experiences before abstract concept exploration should begin (Hobson, 2007). During the 19th and 20th centuries many educators have chosen this practical approach when presenting new concepts to young children. The use of concrete experiences preceding abstract computer activities is one approach to preparing young children to use computers. Children are able to gain necessary computer skills through interaction with games and activities that prepare learners for skills that will be needed when using computers.

Still, Net Generation learners have demonstrated that it is an erroneous assumption that children have to learn simple concepts before difficult ones can be conquered (Whitehead in Chartock, 2000; Kaminski, Sloutsky, & Heckler, 2008). According to Chartock (2000), both Bruner (1975) and Whitehead (1957) believe "if complex ideas are expressed in an appropriate format, a child of any age can learn them" (p. 94). Therefore, two seemingly incongruent concepts are being presented here. The first notion is that concrete experiences should precede abstract activities for young children to grasp new concepts. The games presented in this chapter are one option to achieving this goal. The second precept is that young children can have a leap in understanding and are able to grasp complex concepts even before more basic ideas are fully comprehended. Children raised with computers develop hypertext minds that leap around. It is almost as if cognitive structures are parallel, not sequential (Prensky, 2001b).

The researcher acknowledges that both processes although seemingly in contrast can occur when children interact with computers. Concrete experiences preceding abstract concepts are useful for educators to offer young children. Yet young computer users also have leaps in understanding with complex concepts during computer activity time. The eclectic approach presented here is that young children grasping new computer concepts can be offered hands-on experiences before abstract concepts are understood, but there will be times young children working with computers have a leap in understanding when encountering new concepts.

COMPUTERS AND DEVELOPMENTALLY APPROPRIATE PRACTICE

When forming an educational approach to work with young children and computers, it is important for adults to think about how to do so in a developmentally appropriate manner (NAEYC, 1997). A teacher needs to understand what typically developing children of a certain age are capable of learning as well as providing for the individual unique abilities and skills of each child (NAEYC, 1997). A resource available when thinking about planning developmentally appropriate activities to guide young children with learning about computers is the Technology Position Statement (1996) offered by the NAEYC. NAEYC is an organization:

> dedicated to improving the well-being of all young children, with particular focus on the quality of educational and developmental services for all children from birth through age 8, NAEYC is the world's largest organization working on behalf of young children with nearly 100,000 members, a national network of over 300 local, state, and regional Affiliates, and a growing global alliance of like-minded organizations. (¶ 1)

The complete position statement is presented in Appendix F and offers guidelines for both parents and teachers. In this section the first three statements of the NAEYC (1996) Technology Position Statement that relate to the current study will be discussed in relation to the current study. By connecting the current research results to the NAEYC (1996) Technology Position Statement the developmentally appropriate and practical application of adults guiding young children with computers will be considered. Through this discussion the results of the current research of young children learning about computers in the home setting is linked to the practical approach of adults, whether parents or teachers, guiding children with computers.

1. In evaluating the appropriate use of technology, NAEYC applies principles of developmentally appropriate practice (Bredekamp 1987) and appropriate curriculum and assessment (NAEYC & NAECS/SDE 1992). In short, NAEYC believes that in any given situation, a professional judgment by the teacher is required to determine if a specific use of technology is age appropriate, individually appropriate, and culturally appropriate.

The study parents allowed their children to begin to use computers at the age of 2 or 3. To these adults this young age was appropriate for the children in their families. Most of the children began their computer use in the home setting. Therefore the age appropriateness for initiation with computers was decided by the child's parent. Just as with television program selection or videogame activity choices, these study parents decided when it was age appropriate for their children to begin to use computers.

The parents in the study all offered computer use at a level the parents of each family thought was individually appropriate for the 6-year-old child. The adults' judgment as parents determined when computer use began, which software programs were available for the child to play with, and which, if any, web sites the child was allowed to access. The length of time the children interacted with the home computer was monitored. During the study observations the time on computers for the study children ranged from 30 to 120 minutes. Only one child stopped after 30 minutes and another stayed on the computer one time for 2 hours. For the other 22 visits, computer activity time lasted between 45 and 60 minutes.

Using computers was clearly one of many activity choices offered by the parents for their children. Culturally in these American, Staten Island, New York, homes computers were one of an array of recreational or educational tools. For the study children, other recreational activities in the home setting to choose from were playing with neighborhood friends, arranging playdates with school friends at the study child's home, watching television, playing video games, watching DVDs, reading, drawing, or playing with toys.

When interviewed, the study parents conveyed the use of computers as important but not exclusive as an activity for their children to select. As with other recreational activities the study parents monitored computer time and did not allow the one activity choice to dominate their children's free time. These parents did consider the knowledge of how to use computers as important for their children's future educational and career choices. Study parents did understand that they needed to monitor computer use time and allow for a range of free-time activity choices by their children. The adults in the current study exercised their parental responsibility when determining when it was age appropriate, individually appropriate, and culturally appropriate for their children to use computers.

2. Used appropriately, technology can enhance children's cognitive and social abilities.

When parents were interviewed for the current study the adults discussed the importance of computer knowledge for their children's educational success, future career success, and preparation to maneuver in a world immersed in technology. Li, Atkins, and Stanton (2006) offer Vygotsky's (1962) hypothesis that when computers are programmed with developmentally appropriate, interactive software the mediating tool can serve to scaffold concept development and cognitive performance among young children. By providing assistance to children's learning, computers will act as scaffolding agents and lead to a child's increased cognitive development. The parents in this study understood the importance and significance of computer knowledge for their children and offered their children appropriate access to computers.

The social aspect for computer activity time was when the children used a computer with a partner when visiting at a friend's house or shared their home computer with a friend or sibling at their own home. Five of the six families who participated in the study had two children in the family. Negotiating access to the home computer was a skill that the 6-year-old study children needed to coordinate computer time with siblings. The two study children who had older siblings would at times ask their brothers for assistance when computer hardware or software challenges arose during the child's computer time. During the parent interviews, none of the study parents verbalized a concern about the computer being an isolating tool. The parents did discuss how using the home computer with a friend or sibling did cause the children to work cooperatively.

3. Appropriate technology is integrated into the regular learning environment and used as one of many options to support children's learning.

Computers are capable of providing children with the opportunity to access a world of information, people, and places. By using computers in a developmentally appropriate manner, young children's learning may potentially benefit. When learning new tasks computers can provide assistance, support, and guidance in a manner that fits the learning style of young children. With computers even when a child does not know how to read, a child can enjoy hearing a story. Even with limited geometry skills a child is able to build a house (Judge, Puckett, & Cabuk, 2004). The parents in the research study did choose to use computers to support their children's learning experiences. At times home computers were used by parents to provide assistance with homework assignments or to conduct research to find out about subjects needed to complete school assignments.

Computers were one of many approaches used by study parents to support their children's cognitive development. The children were read to by parents, taken to the library, as well as their parents being involved in knowing what was happening educationally for their children in school. For parents in this study, the use of computers in the home setting supported and enhanced other approaches used to enable the study children to grow intellectually and reinforce learning from the home to the school setting. For example, 6-year-old Ashley was encouraged by her mother, Gina, to use an educational web site offered by the New York City Department of Education which reinforced literacy learning that was occurring in the school setting.

The parents in the current study were using developmentally appropriate approaches to guide their young children during computer activity time. NAEYC (1997) offers guidelines and strategies for adults to understand appropriate approaches for guiding young children learning new concepts. The significance of the study results connect once again to the emergent literacy approach of examining what is successful in the home setting to think about approaches that could be utilized in the school setting.

An educational method that has been used by early childhood educators is to offer young children concrete, hands-on experiences before trying to get children to grasp abstract concepts. For example, a teacher might be guiding children to understand position words such as on, under, in, through, over, beside, right, or left. Comprehension of concept words is required for reading and math skill development. When a teacher tells a child to "Place a check in front of the correct answer," a child cannot complete the task if the terminology related to the concept of directionality is not clear. Hands-on activities allow a child to explore position words to gain an understanding of the abstract concepts related to the words.

When the author was an early childhood educator, the gymnasium was a useful place to teach 3-year-old children about concept words and directionality. An obstacle course could be set up for experimentation with tunnels to go *through* or planks to walk *over*. As children explored an obstacle course, the teachers working with the children would use the concept words to enable the children to learn and understand the words *through* or *over*. Using these hands-on activities the young children were learning position words that would be useful when trying to grasp abstract words encountered during reading or math experiences.

GUIDING EARLY COMPUTER LITERACY

The development of computer literacy is an ongoing process and does not have one point where a parent or teacher is able to state, "Acquisition of computer literacy has begun." A child noticing computers as part of the primary care setting is the beginning of the continual learning process that eventually leads to the attainment of computer literacy. During Early Computer Literacy young children are becoming familiar with what a computer is and how to use a computer. A time when children can be guided to interact with concrete, hands-on activities to understand abstract concepts is when children are 3, 4, or 5 years of age.

Therefore, whether it is a parent, teacher, or an instructor, there are hands-on games and activities that can be offered to promote the concepts needed when using a computer. Adults can play board games with children to help with the discovery of how to follow directions. When lining up to leave the classroom, a teacher can give specific, sequential steps for children to follow. This action is useful to teach children about following a sequence to complete a task. These tangible games and activities assist children in developing skills that will be needed when interacting with computers. The information for the handmade games presented is written as if it was for teachers but is also applicable to parents and instructors. The games and activities presented in this section will guide Early Computer Literacy learners on their journey from concrete to abstract concept development.

Developing Skills in Following Procedures

The author has stated to college students in class that "Computers are machines. If you left your computer turned on and running for weeks and did not press the enter key, the machine would just sit there. You, the human, have to act on the machine that waits for your action to have a reaction." Individuals who understand how to get their desired reaction from the computer are more likely to have a positive computer session. Knowing how to follow procedures for how to use computers enables the person interacting with a computer to proceed and not become frustrated with how to have sustained computer interaction. Being able to follow procedures for using computer hardware, software programs, or Internet browsing, will allow the computer user to have a fruitful experience. There are hands-on games that young children are able to play in the classroom, gymnasium, or playground that offer opportunities to develop skills in understanding how to follow procedures. The skills gained through these classroom activities are useful in working with computers in an abstract world.

Patterned Bracelet

Preparation

Through the activity of making a patterned bracelet, children will learn about following directions. Through this same activity children are also learning to read iconic pictures and develop fine motor skills. All the proficiencies promoted through this activity are beneficial for skills that will be needed when interacting with computers. To prepare for the activity, the teacher will create cards with pictures of the directions that need to be followed. The pictures that need to be made are:

1. A picture of a hand picking up one elastic string.
2. A picture of the hands placing four red beads on the string. (two sets)
3. A picture of the hands placing four white beads on the string. (two sets)
4. A picture of the hands placing four blue beads on the string. (two sets)
5. A picture of the bracelet on a wrist.

Materials for each group of four children

(10) Small bowls
(4) Pieces of 12" elastic string
(50) Each of red, white, and blue beads (wooden or plastic)
(8) Iconic direction pictures
(4) Iconic picture direction sheets

When the bowls are lined up, the first bowl will have the elastic string. The second bowl will have red beads. The third bowl will have white beads. The fourth bowl will have blue beads. For the fifth, sixth, and seventh bowls the red, white, and blue bead colors will be repeated. The picture with the hand wearing the bracelet will be placed on the table next to the last bowl with beads. A direction sheet (using the same pictures placed in front of each bowl) needs to be made for children to follow the directions. The order of the pictures for the direction sheet should be numbered 1–8 and the pictures should be:

1. A picture of a hand picking up an elastic string.
2. A picture of the hands placing four red beads on the string.
3. A picture of the hands placing four white beads on the string.
4. A picture of the hands placing four blue beads on the string.
5. A picture of the hands placing four red beads on the string.
6. A picture of the hands placing four white beads on the string.
7. A picture of the hands placing four blue beads on the string.
8. A picture of the bracelet on a wrist.

Procedure

The teacher will gather a small group of children at the table where the bowls are lined up with the iconic pictures in front of each bowl. The activity would begin with a discussion of what a pattern is. Patterns that could be focused on are patterns in children's clothing, in items around the classroom, or with colored, wooden cubes the teacher brings to the activity. The teacher could then ask how the pictures in front of each bowl might be useful in creating patterned bracelets. Questions that might be asked are: "How many red beads are used for the beginning of the bracelet? What color is used after the first set of red beads? How many colors are used in the pattern?"

After the children grasp the notion of patterns and repeating patterns then they are ready to create their bracelets. The children will each take an empty bowl and will take turns going down the line of supplies and will select what is needed to make their bracelet. The children will then sit with their iconic direction sheet for guidelines on how to make the bracelet. After the bracelets are made the concept of following multistep directions, using iconic pictures, and the use of fine motor skills can be reviewed (depending on which of the concepts were explored during the activity). Questions that could be asked are: "How many steps did you follow to be able to make your bracelet? How did you know how to make your bracelet?" Through this activity the children will have hands-on experience following multistep directions which is a skill children need when using computers.

Making a Peanut Butter and Jelly Sandwich

Preparation

The teacher will gather the supplies needed for the recipe and prepare the work area to complete the recipe with four children at a time. There are two options for how the children will follow the sequential recipe. The first option is to have the numbered recipe on an enlarged piece of chart paper and to post the recipe by the table where the children will be working. The second option would be to have the recipe written on an 8 ½" X 10" piece of paper and give a copy to each child. Either approach would work for this activity to guide children to develop skills for following directions. Set up each of the four place settings with a 9" plate, a folded napkin, and a plastic knife and plastic spoon placed on the napkin. One bowl of peanut butter and one bowl of jelly would be placed in front of each child. As with any cooking activity, be sure to check children's food allergies and plan accordingly. If any children have a peanut allergy then the peanut butter can be changed to cream cheese, bananas, or another food choice.

Materials for each group of four children

- (8) Slices of multigrain bread
- (4) Small bowls of peanut butter
- (4) Small bowls of grape jelly (or strawberry)
- (4) Plastic knives
- (4) 9" Plastic plates
- (4) Napkins

Procedure

The cold cooking activity would begin with the children first washing their hands. When the children are seated at the table, explain to them that they will each be making their own peanut butter and jelly sandwiches. To make each sandwich the recipe will be followed in the order it is written so that each child creates his or her own special and delicious sandwich. For step one have each child select two slices of bread and place the bread on their plate. For step two the children will use their spoon to scoop two spoonfuls of jelly onto one slice of bread. In step three the knife will be used to place two smears of peanut butter onto the other slice of bread. The final step is that the two slices of bread are pressed together. The peanut butter and jelly sandwich is now ready to eat.

During the procedure the teacher can ask questions to focus the children's attention on the numbered recipe. Questions that can be asked are: "What do we have to do first to make the sandwich? What is step three? In which step do we use our spoon to get jelly for the sandwich?" By focusing on the sequential order of the recipe the children are able to explore the concept of following a sequential procedure to complete a task. The skills developed during this cooking activity will be of use when interacting with a computer.

Obstacle Course Using Iconic Pictures

Preparation

To prepare for an obstacle course, the teacher would have to decide which equipment would work best for a visual explanation of how to complete the activity. The pictures can be created with a digital camera using photographs that show a child completing each of the activities. For example, a picture can be taken of a child rolling down sideways on the incline mat. The options for the activities can be decided by selecting from the equipment at the school that is available for the children to use.

Set up the gym area for the activity by placing the four pieces of equipment with the corresponding picture behind each apparatus. Space the equipment apart enough that the child has room to move from the piece of equipment just used and to have space to be ready to try the next piece of equipment. For the activity described in this example, first a picture of a child rolling down the incline mat is placed on the floor at the high end of the mat. Next, a picture of a child bouncing on a hop ball is placed on the floor by the hop ball starting location. The picture of a child walking across the low balance beam is placed on the floor at the front of the beam. At the end of the balance beam, by the playground ball, place a picture of a child bouncing the ball.

Materials for each child

    (1) 3' X 6' Incline mat
    (1) Hop ball
    (1) 6' X 2.8" balance beam
    (1) 8.5" Playground ball
    (4) Laminated iconic direction pictures

Procedure

For this particular gym obstacle course iconic pictures of an incline mat, hop ball, balance beam, and playground ball will be used. The 8" X 10" pictures of each action that will be completed with the equipment are placed on the floor next to the apparatus. Before beginning the activity, the teacher will explain to the group of children that they will be completing the obstacle course by following the directions on the pictures that are placed by each obstacle. The teacher will walk with the group to the incline mat and might ask "How do we know what to do here? What will you have to do when you come here?" After walking as a group to each obstacle in the course and discussing the action to be taken, the children will line up and each child will have a turn completing the course. An adult should be placed at each stop of the obstacle course. The adults will guide the children to look at the picture as a reminder of what needs to be done with the gym equipment.

    To complete the obstacle course, first a child would begin by rolling down the incline mat. Next there would be a hop ball placed near the bottom of the incline mat with a picture of a child hopping toward the balance beam. Then there would be a picture at the front of the balance beam of a child walking across the beam. At the end of the balance beam there would be a picture of a child bouncing a ball to the red tape on the floor which is the finish line of the obstacle course. During the activity each time a child completes the obstacle course, an adult has to return the balls back to the starting location to be ready for the next child completing the course. When all the children have completed the obstacle course the group can be gathered together once more. The teacher will review the concept of iconic pictures and how by using the pictures, the obstacle course instructions were understood. The group might be able to brainstorm what other instructions can be given using iconic pictures.

Developing Skills for Using a Limited Menu

When using a computer software program or a web site, there are choices and options to select when deciding what to do next. A child needs to learn about making choices from the limited options on a computer screen. In an earlier activity, a recipe was used to develop children's ability to follow procedures. A recipe can also be used to prepare children to understand about making choices from a limited selection on a menu. By gaining hands-on, concrete experiences during play, a young child will gain an understanding about how to choose from items being offered. If a fruit salad recipe offers the choices of bananas, oranges, or blueberries, then the children are not able to select apples. The children must choose from the items available. The knowledge of understanding about choosing from a limited menu will be useful when interacting with computer software programs or Internet web sites.

Activity: Fruit Salad for One

Preparation

The cold cooking instructions for this recipe-for-one activity are set up so each child is able to independently create his or her own dish to eat. To prepare for the activity an adult would gather the fruit and other materials that will be needed. In this sample recipe fruit choices include oranges, bananas, and blueberries. The different fruits are each cut into slices or bite-size pieces and are each placed in small salad bowls: oranges in one bowl, bananas in another, and blueberries in a third bowl. Two tables are needed for the activity. One table is where the children will sit and talk with the teacher about the activity and will sit to eat the fruit salad made. The other table is where the fruit choices are set up in a straight line. The sequence for the items is small salad bowls, spoons, one bowl for each cut-up fruit item, and napkins.

Materials for each group of four children

> Pint of blueberries
> (2) Oranges
> (2) Bananas
> (8) Bowls
> (8) Spoons
> (4) Fruit Salad Menu sheets
> (4) Pencils
> Napkins

Procedure

The activity would be presented by the teacher in small groups of four children at a time. An appropriate time for the activity would be during free playtime as the class is busy with center activities. The teacher is able to discuss the concept of selecting from a limited menu with four children

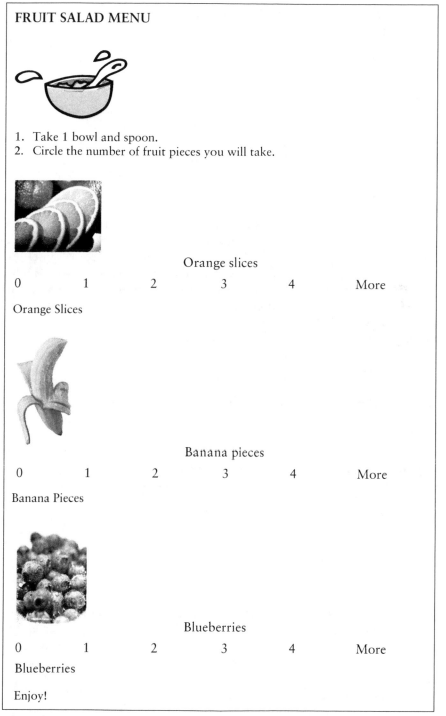

FRUIT SALAD MENU

1. Take 1 bowl and spoon.
2. Circle the number of fruit pieces you will take.

Orange slices

| 0 | 1 | 2 | 3 | 4 | More |

Orange Slices

Banana pieces

| 0 | 1 | 2 | 3 | 4 | More |

Banana Pieces

Blueberries

| 0 | 1 | 2 | 3 | 4 | More |

Blueberries

Enjoy!

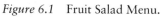

Figure 6.1 Fruit Salad Menu.

at a time at the table designated for the activity. First the concept of choosing from the items available for the recipe would be discussed. Each child would be given a copy of the Fruit Salad Menu sheet (see Figure 6.1) and a pencil. Questions will be asked to enable the children to focus on the concept of what a limited menu actually is. Questions that could be asked include "What are the fruit choices on this menu? Can you choose items that are *not* on the menu? Can you choose strawberries?" If strawberries are not one of the fruits offered on the menu then children are made aware that they could not choose that menu item. Through discussion the children will begin to understand the meaning of *selecting from a limited menu*. During the recipe-for-one activity, computers are not discussed and the child is not made aware of the connection of concrete skills for development of abstract understanding.

The children would be guided to circle their choices of fruit that they will select when they make their fruit salad. Next, one at a time, each child takes the completed menu sheet to the activity table and begins by selecting a bowl and spoon. Each child would walk along the line of fruit bowls and would select the number of pieces chosen for each fruit that was circled on their own menu sheet. After making their fruit salad following their selected recipe the children would eat their fruit salads. The activity could conclude with a review of possible items that could not have been chosen and what was chosen.

A variation on this limited menu activity used by the author for many years is making a Me-Salad. For this salad recipe a 9" plate and salad ingredients are chosen. Items could include shredded lettuce, sliced cucumbers, cherry tomatoes, black olives, diced carrots, or green olives. A menu sheet would be prepared for the children to use as was done in the fruit salad activity. The teacher would again talk to the children about the concept of selecting from a menu of items. The idea of what our faces look like is also discussed. The children are then instructed to choose ingredients from the choices available to make a salad on their own plate that looks like their individual faces.

Activity: Book Gizmo

Preparation

Another activity that gives children experience with interacting with a limited menu is the *Book Gizmo*. An empty refrigerator box or other large-size cardboard box is converted to resemble a vending machine. A large opening will be cut into the back of the box. The panel opposite the large opening will be the front of the machine. The box will be placed with the large opening facing a wall so the chair placed inside the box where a child or teacher is sitting will not be visible to the class. The person who sits inside the box on the chair is the book vendor. The front panel of the box

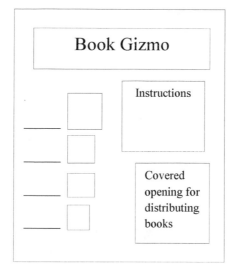

Figure 6.2   Book Gizmo.

is decorated with the title *Book Gizmo* (see Figure 6.2). Four openings are cut along the left front of the box where the selection coins are inserted. Pictures of each of the four book selections will be attached to the right of the cutout coin slot. The instruction sheet is also placed onto the front of the machine. An opening is cut out on the right side of the front panel, large enough for the book selected to be handed through the covered opening. The opening can be covered with a piece of material attached to the top of the hole. This will keep the children from being able to see the person behind the machine. You will need four copies of each book title being offered as supplies for the machine.

A collection of coins placed in a basket by the machine will be needed. The coins can be made by tracing 3-inch circles on cardboard, cutting out the circles, and then decorating the coins. Four of the coins need to have "Make another choice" on the coin for when there are no more books of one title available. The coins created should be laminated to be more durable. To be able to dispense books from the Book Gizmo, a chair needs to be placed behind the vending machine. During playtime, an adult or child will sit on the chair. As coins are placed in slots, the vendor needs to notice which slot the coin was placed in and will then hand the book chosen through the covered opening. To be able to collect books that have been read, a tray is placed on the floor next to the box.

There are many possible variations on this limited menu activity that could be used instead of books. The menu could offer different stuffed animals or different color choices for Unifix cubes. For the limited menu choices, words or picture icons can be used for the selection items. If the activity will be used with different items then a plastic sheet should be placed next to each slot so pictures for the items used can be placed in the sleeve. Through experimentation with the book device, children will learn that they can select from a limited menu and are developing menu reading skills.

Materials for each group of four children

(1) Empty cardboard box approximately 30" length X 36" width X 72" height
(4) Each of four different children's books for a total of 16 books
(1) Picture of each book
(20) Coins
(1) Basket
(1) Tray
(1) Instruction sheet with iconic instructions

Procedure

The activity should first be introduced during Circle Time. The teacher will explain what the machine is and the concept of selecting items from a limited menu. Children should be given turns trying out the machine and becoming familiar with the procedure. Remind children about placing the coins into the book choice slots and placing books read in the return tray next to the vending machine. The children will be told that Book Gizmo will be available during Free Playtime for their enjoyment.

During the first time the machine is available during Free Playtime, a teacher should monitor the vending machine activity and guide children as needed. Questions that might be asked include: "Which book choices do you see? What is one of the books on the menu?" Children might need to be reminded to return the books to the tray after they have finished reading. If this is not done then the machine will quickly run out of supplies. Discussion of Book Gizmo can occur during Circle Time to reinforce the concept of selecting from a limited menu.

Keyboard Skills

Using a keyboard is one option to input information into a computer. The arrangement of the rows of letters on the keys was developed in the 1860s when the typewriter was first invented. Notice the top left row of letters on the computer keyboard diagram here. The name of the QWERTY keyboard was chosen from the arrangement of these typewriter keys and is the keyboard style still used today (Hartcourt Education Company, 2007).

The original reason for the arrangement of the letter pads on a typewriter was so that a person typing quickly would not have two rods for the

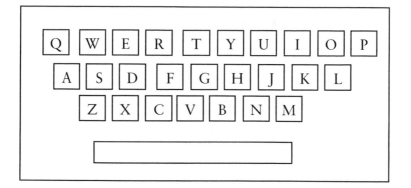

Figure 6.3 QWERTY keyboard.

letters striking together and jamming the machine. With computers no such collision of letters is a concern yet the QWERTY keyboard is still the one chosen most. Children need to become accustomed to looking for letters on a computer keyboard. Playing games with enlarged keyboard letters will assist with this task.

Activity: Keyboard Hop

Preparation

To create the keyboard hop mat, each capital letter of the alphabet will be printed on the underside of a 45" X 53" nonskid, clear mat for hard floors. The mat must be used on a bare floor as it would slide on a carpeted floor. The letters need to be drawn on the bottom of the mat so they do not fade from children jumping on the mat. The letters will be printed with permanent marker and written in the same order as the sample QWERTY keyboard in this chapter. Only the letters of the alphabet will be used, not any numbers or other keys. A rectangular shape which is the space bar will be drawn under the letters. When the letters are printed on the bottom of the clear mat, they must be written in reverse order to appear correctly when the mat is flipped over and placed on the floor. Be sure to check that the mat stays in place for the children's safety. Do not use this activity if you cannot get a clear, nonskid floor mat that remains stationary.

A set of word cards is made and placed in a tray. The game is played with partners. The procedure for the game is:

1. Child A selects a word from the tray.

2. Child A reads the word and then hands the word card to Child B.
3. Child A will stand on the rectangular starting point (the space bar of the keyboard) to begin.
4. Child B reads the word again.
5. Child A will hop from letter to letter to spell the word.
6. Child B checks to be sure Child A is hopping to the correct letters.
7. After the word is spelled Child A says the word again.
8. Now it is Child B's turn to select a word and hop to spell.
9. Play continues until all the words in the tray have been read and spelled.

Materials for Floor Mat

(1) Tray
(20) Word cards—a collection of laminated, printed words
(1) 45" X 53" nonskid, clear mat

Procedure

To explain the game to children, introduce the activity during Circle Time. Explain to the class that each letter of the alphabet is written one time on this display. Tell the class that words they may know are available in the tray for them to pick and then hop on each letter to spell out the entire word. Let the children know that as they become more experienced they can actually spell out a complete sentence by jumping from letter to letter. Let a few of the children take turns trying the activity by selecting a word from the tray, standing on the rectangle (the space bar), and then hopping from letter to letter, in correct order, to spell the word. Let the class know the game will be available during Free Play-time to try independently.

Questions that might be asked by the teacher during the activity are: "What are the first five letters above the row that begins with the letter "A?" (the answer is QWERTY and the children can be told this type of keyboard is called a QWERTY keyboard), or "I have the word *cat* here, who would like to try to hop on each letter to spell the word?" The connection of the keyboard to the computer can be explained but doing so is not required for the activity. The children will need time and numerous opportunities for experimentation to become familiar with the placement of the letters on the board.

A variation of the keyboard jumping game is to use a 16" X 14" metal cookie sheet and to draw 1" square keyboard letters on the tray. Create a second set of 1" square laminated alphabet letters that have magnets on the back of each letter. The letters would be placed in a tray. Another tray will have laminated printed sets of words. To play the game a child would select a word from the tray, select the correct letters, and place the magnet letters onto the cookie sheet. Through their exploration, children will become more familiar with the placement of letters on a keyboard.

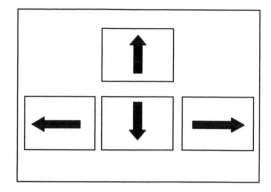

Figure 6.4   Arrow key pad.

Activity: Gym Obstacle Course to Understand Directionality

When using a computer keyboard there may be times a computer user has to use the arrow key pad (see Figure 6.4) to move the computer cursor on the screen either up, down, to the right, or to the left. To understand the concept of directionality, children are able to experiment with following directions by completing an obstacle course during gym time.

Preparation

To prepare for this activity a teacher will select various gym equipment that will be set up to form a four-step obstacle course. For example, a mat, low balance beam, 8" playground ball, and tricycle will be placed around the gym. By using down directional mats from one piece of gym equipment to the next, the child will proceed in the direction each arrow indicates to

Figure 6.5   Straight downward directional arrow.

complete the course. Directional arrow sheets can be made using a word processing software program or with directional mats purchased from a children's gym equipment supplier. Figure 6.5 is an example of a directional arrow a teacher is able to create. Each arrow drawing would cover an entire 8 ½" X 11" sheet of paper.

For the obstacle course described here, first the child would begin at the 6' mat. Three straight arrow mats will be placed 2' apart from the end of the mat to the beginning of the balance beam. Next, place three arrows 2' apart from the balance beam to the tricycle. In front of the tricycle place six arrows from the tricycle to where the playground ball is placed on the ground 15–20' away. Finally place three arrows 2' apart from the playground ball to the end of the course where a finish line is placed on the ground.

Since this activity might be used as one of the first activities to have children experiment with directionality, the basic concept of the arrow is being explored. All the arrows would be facing in one direction. In future obstacle courses, different directions can be utilized in the same obstacle course to enable children to gain an understanding of all the directions on the arrow key pad. Through this concrete, hands-on exploration of following a downward arrow children are gaining skills that will be needed for the abstract concepts that will be encountered when using computers.

Materials

(1) 6' gym mat
(1) 6' X 2.8" Balance beam
(1) Tricycle
(1) 8 ½" Playground ball
(12) Straight arrow mats
(2) Pieces of removable tape, one labeled "Starting Line" one labeled "Finish Line"

Procedure

This activity will be introduced to the children as a class before the children try the obstacle course individually. The teacher will have the course set up and will start by gathering the children at the gym mat with the tape on the floor labeled "Starting Line." The teacher will explain that the children will begin by walking across the mat in the direction that the footprints are facing. After getting to the end of the mat, the children will be instructed to follow the arrows to the next piece of equipment, the balance beam. The children will be told to walk across the balance beam and to follow the arrows on the floor at the end of the beam until they get to the tricycle. They will ride the tricycle until they reach the ball. Finally they will bounce the ball in the direction of the arrows, until they arrive at the finish line, which means they have completed the obstacle course. Questions that can be asked during the introduction of the activity are: "How do you know which way to go on the obstacle course? Which way do all the arrows point?"

When the children are completing the obstacle course, there needs to be an adult at the starting line to pace the children beginning. There also needs to be an adult at each of the equipment stations for safety, to pace the children, and to set up the equipment as needed after children have passed the station. The adults can offer verbal guidance if a child has forgotten what needs to be done with the equipment at each station. The children can be reminded to look at the arrows if they are unsure which way to go. After all of the children have participated with completing the obstacle course once or twice, gather the group together to review the concept of directionality once more. Ask the children, "How did you know which way to go?" Have a discussion about how the arrows prevent children using the equipment from bumping into each other and how the arrows are useful to tell the children which direction to go.

Fine Motor Skills

In order to successfully use a computer mouse, touch screen, or stylus, young children need to have control of their fine motor skill abilities. There are a variety of possible activities which will promote fine motor skill development. Activities for young children might include using clay, pencils, paintbrushes, puzzles, chalk, cutting with scissors, turning the pages of a book, or pinching a clothespin open to hang artwork to dry. The play dough recipe that follows would offer opportunities to promote fine motor skill development, as well as practice with the following procedures. The author has been using this basic recipe with young children and preservice teachers for 20 years.

Activity: Homemade Play Dough

Recipe:

  4 cups flour
  ¼ cup of salt
  1 ½ cups of warm water
  3 drops food coloring
  1 tablespoon oil
  2 mixing bowls

In one bowl mix together the flour and salt. In another bowl mix the water, oil, and food coloring together. Gradually stir the dry and wet ingredients together. Knead the mixture as you add the liquid ingredients. Add more water if the dough is too stiff, or add more flour if the dough is too sticky. This recipe can be made by an adult and children together with the grown-up taking the lead for correctly completing the recipe. There are many variations that can be used for this basic recipe. Variations include adding paint instead of food coloring, adding a small quantity of coffee grounds to the mixture for texture, or adding cinnamon for a fragrant scent. Using the play dough will allow children to develop manual dexterity skills.

The recreational activities offered in this chapter would provide young children with hands-on, concrete experiences that assist in developing an understanding of more abstract concepts that will be needed when interacting with computers. As a young child's understanding of computers grows during Early Computer Literacy, activities that guide the child's transmission from concrete to abstract notions support the learning experience. By presenting these games to young children, early childhood educators or parents are able to guide the development of a young child's emerging computer literacy skills.

7 Summary, Issues, and Future Research Needs

Parents and teachers grapple with the daunting task of preparing today's children to be tomorrow's citizens, equipped to thrive in a technologically changing, culturally diverse, and intellectually demanding world. Guiding children to become computer literate is a journey that begins when children are very young and continues until independent computer skills are attained. The current research study offers strategies parents used in the home setting to scaffold young children's emergent computer knowledge. Lessons learned from how parents guide children in the home setting might be considered for approaches teachers could utilize in the school setting.

Sally Bowman Alden, Executive Director of the Computer Learning Foundation (2008) posed a valid technology question, "How can parents and teachers encourage children to become computer literate and prepare them for the 21st century?" (¶ 28). Although children growing up with computers are more comfortable with the technology, as with any skill, not all individuals will progress at the same rate. Some children will naturally understand and be willing to engage with computers and other children will be hesitant. Therefore, access to computers and guiding acquisition of computer skills are essential topics to consider jointly when facilitating children's computer literacy.

The children studied in the current research are from the generation known as Generation Y, or the Millennials: people born from 1982 through 1999 (Center for Digital Education, 2007). Generation Y children and young adults have had more opportunities to have access and interaction with computers than previous generations such as Baby Boomers. Subsequently the children of Generation Y have developed more of a comfort with using computers. Children born from 2001 through 2021 are the generation known as Generation Z (Urban Dictionary, 2008). Computer technology has surrounded the daily lives of Generation Z children from infancy. This is the first generation to have computers as part of their educational experience from as early as preschool or kindergarten. If given the essential opportunities required, Generation Z will be exposed to computers as a tool for learning, creativity, productivity, research, communications, and entertainment (Bowman Alden, 2008).

This chapter will review the research results of young children and computers. A sampling of contemporary issues surrounding computers and children in American society will also be addressed. Throughout the discussion, the need for related relevant research will be brought to light. Computers as a field of study incessantly changes as computer hardware, software, and the Internet continually transform and evolve. Understanding what computer literacy is and how the skill emerges within a child is a transformative chameleon that is a challenge to comprehend.

STUDY REVIEW

There are few research studies that focus on the subject of computers and young children in the home setting. There is a critical need for research that examines computer knowledge as the skill develops through young children and their parents interacting with computers in the home setting. In the current study the term *computer* (TechTerms.com, 2008) refers to a desktop, laptop, or tablet computer. In this study the computers that were used by the 6-year-old children were all desktop computers. By adapting an emergent skills approach to studying the issue of how adults guide young children learning to use computers, the significance of the research outcomes becomes evident. How parents guide their children in the home setting has implications for approaches teachers might utilize in the school setting.

The collection and analysis of the data allowed the three research questions of the study to be considered:

1. What strategies do these parents utilize to offer their children guidance and access to computers?
2. What language categories and patterns do these parents utilize to guide their young children interacting with computers?
3. What do these parents consider the significance of computers in their children's lives and what are common goals for their children's acquisition of computer knowledge?

This research offered a qualitative/quantitative approach for observation of parents with their 6-year-old children at the home computer. The current study chose to emulate the methodology of observation that was used by researchers in studies of parents guiding the literacy development of their young children in the home setting (Dickinson & Tabors, 2001; Storch & Whitehurst, 2001; Teale, 1986). Six families participated in the study, with seven parents and six 6-year-old children being observed during four scheduled site visits per child. Videotape recordings, handwritten field notes, and transcriptions of parent interviews and site visits allowed triangulation of data to be achieved. The study results offered a multitude of data to be able to respond to the three research questions.

Question one of the study was: What strategies do these parents utilize to offer their children guidance and access to computers? For the question of guidance, one strategy parents used was to be in close proximity. Another approach used by study parents to offer guidance was consistently providing a verbal response when their children asked for assistance with computer challenges. First the parents would offer a verbal response and then an action would be taken. If the parent was in close proximity help was almost instantaneous. If a parent had to move closer to where the child was to offer assistance then the adult would come closer after a verbal response was given.

Since the study was considering computer use in the home setting, a factor for a family to participate in the study was computer ownership. For the six families there was at least one computer in the home setting. The 6-year-old study children were all permitted access to and use of a home computer. Five of the six children in the study had initial exposure to computers at home when they were 2 or 3 years of age. Parents provided their children with access to computers in various locations besides the home: the library, after-school programs, or when visiting friends or grandparents. All of the study parents viewed computers as an important, educational tool that their children needed a working knowledge of to be able to succeed in school and for career prospects.

Question two of the study asked: What language categories and patterns do these parents utilize to guide their young children interacting with computers? Through detailed scrutiny of study videotapes, observer field notes, and resulting transcriptions the repetitive words, phrases, and actions of parents surfaced. Study parents used language as a tool to scaffold their children's learning at the computer. The language categories for parents talking with their children at the computer were conversational language, directive language, inquiry language, procedural language, and validating language. The main adult language category for study parents talking to their children was conversational language (51%). For conversational language talk was either social talk or computer-related with 96% of adult conversational language being computer-related.

In the current study parent-child discourse was considered to be when a parent and child talked while the child was at the computer. To examine the discourse of parents talking to their children at the computer the discourse coding categories utilized were parent inquiry (PI), child inquiry (CI), mother discussion (MD), and child discussion (CD). When analyzing parent-child discourse, the category of discussion, at 61%, was foremost for parent-child talk at the computer.

When study children verbally requested assistance from a parent a verbal response was given to the child. This was a consistent action taken by parents as the adult moved within closer proximity to the child. Study parents were in close proximity of 1–5 feet, general close proximity of 1–7 feet, or not-in-close proximity of 8 feet or further from where a child was interacting with a computer. Families 1, 2, and 3 had parents who were in general close proximity and for Families 4, 5, and 6 parents were not-in-close proximity during site visit observations. A pattern that emerged from analysis of the data was that parent proximity to children had an impact on quantity of parent-child discourse during the children's interaction with the home computer. Study parents all demonstrated the characteristics of offering their children computer-related conversation, being consistent in verbally responding to their children, and moving within close proximity when guiding their children during home computer activity time.

Parents were asked 20 interview questions with the results being videotaped and transcribed. Parental actions were also observed for four site visits to the six study families. The resulting data provided a wealth of information to be able to explore research question three: What do these parents consider the significance of computers in their children's lives and what are common goals for their children's acquisition of computer knowledge? In parent responses to interview questions, the significance of computers for their children's academic and future career success was revealed. Study parents were all in agreement that their young children need to know how to use a computer. Parents' actions were congruous with their viewpoint as children were given opportunities for computer access at home, at the local library, or by participation in an after-school computer class. Through the use of home computers, school computers, or computers at the library, parents were providing their 6-year-old children with chances to build their knowledge of how to use computers.

Another goal that was evident from parent responses to interview questions was that all study parents want their children to be capable of using computers independently. The six study children would ask parents for assistance when computer challenges were encountered. After parents provided guidance the child was encouraged to continue to independently interact with the computer. For these parents guiding their children with computers in the home setting, their children gaining computer knowledge is an ongoing process and an objective for the learning experience.

One of the queries posed when contemplating this study was: Is the Apprenticeship Model used by these parents to teach their children about computers? Were the study parents the master teachers and their children novices being trained? Parents did use directive language or procedural language and at times told their children what actions to take when using the home computer. Study parents were role models to their children as the adults demonstrated how to solve problems with computer challenges involving computer hardware, computer software, or when Internet difficulties arose. During the current study the researcher focused on the children's behaviors, not the adults'. The researcher did not observe evidence of apprenticeship occurring but more so role modeling of actions that children could emulate when using computers.

The current study was situated in the home setting and focused on parents guiding young children using computers. There were six participant families involved in the study which is an extremely limited population sample. Nonetheless, the study results present a wealth of information to consider when delving into the subject of how adults guide young children using computers. The study results of how parents offer access and guidance for children with computers in the home setting has implications for teachers scaffolding children with computers in the school setting.

COMPUTERS IN THE HOME SETTING

Emergent Computer Skills and the Home Environment

The emergence of literacy in young children has been examined by researchers considering the impact of children's home environments and the influence of parents on emerging literacy skills (Northwest Territories Literacy Council, 2008; Taylor & Dorsey-Gaines, 1988; Teale, 1986; Webster & Feiler, 1998; Wiegel, Martin, & Bennett, 2006). Storch and Whitehurst's (2001) research study offers a detailed view of the impact of parental influences and home environments on young children's literacy development. Storch and Whitehurst adapt Whitehurst and Lonigan's (1998) perspective when viewing the developmental continuum of emergent literacy to include "the skills, knowledge, and attitudes that are developmental precursors to reading and writing and the environments that support these developments" (p. 53).

In the Home-School Study of Language and Literacy Development that began in 1987, a team of researchers used home visits to supplement data collection in trying to understand how language and literacy skills emerge in young children (Dickinson & Tabors, 2001). Observing mothers reading to preschoolers at home and the availability of books in the home setting have allowed researchers to understand the impact of parental guidance and access for literacy opportunities (Dickinson & Tabors, 2001). The same approach is needed in understanding the emergence of computer literacy. Observing what parents do to guide their young children at the computer or the ways in which they offer computer access will reveal the children's possible development of positive dispositions towards the kind of technological applications that will be experienced in the future (Siraj-Blatchford & Whitebread, 2000). Positive experiences in the home setting will prepare children with computer knowledge and possibly an eagerness to interact with computers in the school setting. Further research which focuses on the emergence of computer skills in the home and school settings will enable an understanding of computer attitudes and aptitudes in young children.

Talk at the Computer

When examining talk that occurred at the computer the discourse participants for the current study were the 6-year-old children and their parents. The analysis of the discourse patterns that surfaced raise numerous questions relating to talk at the computer. Did the similar discourse pattern for Family 1 and Family 3 (see Table 4.8) of PD-CD-PI-CI-CR-PR-PF occur by chance for the two families with parents in close proximity? Are the rank order discourse categories for the two families of discussion, inquiry, and response due to the child-centered environment that existed in the home setting? Would such a child-centered approach benefit young children in a school setting? Resulting data might offer possibilities for how teachers could effectively guide children by encouraging certain discourse categories at the computer. Further research of *talk at the computer* both in the home and school settings would serve to examine discourse similarities or differences in the two settings and the impact on children's learning.

The inclusion of a computer program was not part of the language reviewed, as this study focused on the talk between parent and child. The computer program as part of discourse occurring at the computer was explored by Cazden (2001) with two students and a computer program as part of the dynamics being examined. The computer as part of the social and learning dynamic needs to be explored further to understand the quantity, quality, and impact that computer-generated talk has on a child's actions and reactions during computer activity time.

Family Computer Ownership and Dispersion of New Technologies

The home computers that were available to the children in the study ranged from a basic older computer that only functioned to operate software programs to newer computers that could offer access to the Internet. The computers available were family computers used by siblings and parents that were not purchased solely for use by the 6-year-old study children. In the home setting there was a parent available as a resource to try to resolve computer-related challenges for the 6-year-old children. The implication is that when there is a parent with basic computer knowledge available in the home setting, there is an opportunity for a young child to be guided at a home computer and have sustained computer interaction. As family computer ownership increases, the implication is that many young children entering elementary school will have had prior experience with computers. The propensity and capability of young children's encounters with computers will set the tone and direction for teachers to offer appropriate computer activities for children who have had prior knowledge and experience with computers.

Parents in the study all owned a home computer. The issue of a family owning a home computer is one that is impacted by a range of factors.

Researchers considering the role and use of computers by children in American society have examined the impact of family resources (Becker, 2000; Shields & Behrman, 2000; Shonkoff & Phillips, 2000). There are various family dynamics that influence whether or not a young child is able to interact with a home computer such as the number of family members living in the household, if parents are married or divorced, the jobs parents have, the number of hours parents work each week, as well as the number, age, and gender of siblings. These factors will affect the quality and quantity of possible computer resources parents might be able to provide for children in a home setting. In one household having a computer for the family may be a nonessential luxury that is not feasible to purchase. In another household there may be more than one home computer available for use by family members. Parents' financial resources will be a factor in deciding whether or not a computer is part of the home environment.

According to the United States Census Bureau's Current Population Survey (CPS) in 2003 of families with children ages 3–17, 41.9% of families with annual incomes of $20,000–$29,999 and 89.8% of households with family incomes above $75,000–$99,999 have home computers. "Income, education and ethnicity are strong indicators of whether or not children have access to a home computer, as well as strong predictors of the quality of access" (Becker, 2000, p. 59). The financial resources available to children from affluent families offer the advantage of being exposed to computers and having gained computer skills before beginning school. Shonkoff and Phillips (2000) state that "features of families account for sizeable differences in the learning opportunities that children are exposed to prior to school entry and, in turn, for the wide disparities in knowledge and abilities that characterize kindergarteners" (p. 157). Families that are disadvantaged, socially and economically, will face exclusion from the computer revolution engulfing society (Attewell, Suazo-Garcia, & Battle, 2003).

Peer Scaffolding

At times for Family 2 and Family 4 there was a sibling in the area who offered to assist or did sit with their sibling to assist during computer activity. The focus of the current study was parents and their 6-year-old children. Therefore, the dynamics and activities that occurred between the two 6-year-old girls and their 8-year-old brothers were not discussed for the current study. The other three families with siblings each had one sibling younger than the 6-year-old study child. One of the 6-year-old girls had a 4-year-old sister, for the two 6-year-old boys there was one with a 4-year-old brother, and the other had a 4-year-old sister. None of the 6-year-old children did seek assistance from their younger siblings. The interactions and impact of siblings in the home setting with computers is a topic that needs further research.

During the interviews, parents in the study discussed how the 6-year-old children played at the computer socially with friends at their own home or when visiting their friends' homes. Cooperative learning that occurred during playtime at the computer was not considered in the current study, yet peer guidance at the computer is an issue that has importance for learning in the home and school setting. Research is needed that examines if the same strategies adults use when guiding children are the approaches peers use to guide contemporaries at the computer.

COMPUTERS IN THE SCHOOL SETTING

Two of the children in the research study were attending a local Staten Island, New York, public elementary school where classes were assigned either computer time or gym time. Time and resources did not allow the school to offer all the classes in the school access to computers as part of the school curriculum. Time, space, and finances present barriers for access to computers for many children in schools. Boitnott (2007) stated the crux of the computer issue when declaring "Computers are here to stay and are going to remain part of the landscape of our society into the foreseeable future. We owe it to our young people to prepare them for the digital age that awaits them in the world of work" (¶ 12). To acquire computer literacy it is essential that children have access to computers in the school setting (Armstrong & Casement, 2000).

Teachers in American schools need to educate students about computers and the connection to being prepared for future work opportunities. The message teachers need to convey to students is that all jobs, including those in literature, the arts, medicine, design, law, as well as the helping professions, will require computer knowledge (American Association of University Women [AAUW], 2000). Since passage of the *No Child Left Behind Act* (2001) teachers are faced with competing instructional priorities and pressure to prepare their students to pass standardized state tests. Within the NCLB framework, teachers view support for innovative instructional design as being needed if technology is to be effectively infused into students' learning experiences (Davis, Fuller, Jackson, Pittman, & Sweet, 2007).

The current study is a beginning step toward understanding how parents and adults are able to guide young children in understanding how to use computers. The study results reveal the positive impact of an adult offering a child computer access, being in close proximity to a child using a computer, and the importance of talk to guide a child's computer experience. Study parents offered their children opportunities for experimentation and discovery when using computers in the home setting. With direct guidance from parents and chances for independent computer activity time, these children are building their computer knowledge.

Readiness Approach and Computers

In the 1930s the educational perspective for literacy was that young children were not mentally ready for instruction of learning to read and write until they were chronologically 6 and a half years old (Slegers, 1996). This maturational approach to reading and writing was known as the Readiness Model. The readiness viewpoint considered the skills of reading and writing as developing separately. When offering instruction to a young child, "Teachers were advised not to tamper with the unfolding maturation of the child" (p. 6). Even though there was no research to support the readiness approach, this methodology for teaching reading and writing persisted until the 1970s and 1980s.

Marie Clay (1966) was one of the pioneers who introduced the perspective that reading and writing were not separate skills to be learned but the two were intertwined as children became literate. She coined the phrase *emergent literacy* and was a proponent of the concept that literacy skills emerge over a child's lifetime from birth on. The inaccuracy of the maturational viewpoint that a child needed to be 6 and a half years of age to begin to learn was recognized. It was realized that a child being actively engaged in the process of reading and writing does not have a single point of origin but is an ongoing process.

This background information for the Reading Readiness Model (Slegers, 1996) is presented because the same approach is being suggested for young children learning to use computers in the school setting. The analogy of computer literacy skills with the emergence approach for literacy skills is valid in this discussion as well. This research purports that there should not be a predetermined and set older age when children should be allowed to begin to use computers. Anyone who is present when a 2-year-old tries to use a parent's cell phone can attest to the interest and ability of a child trying to interact with technology tools. Many adults who first began to use computers as teenagers or adults are hesitant when initially trying to use new technology tools. The author has worked with adults who are cautious when first working with computers and whose attitude is "I am afraid I will break it." The researcher has noted that young children observed during the research study did not have such trepidation.

In 2006 the researcher had conducted site visits to observe college students in Manhattan, New York, schools. One of the schools visited was a private elementary school. The school offers an excellent developmentally appropriate educational experience for elementary age students. The instructional approach for incorporating computers into the curriculum was discussed with the program director. The school chooses to wait until third grade to include computers as part of the program syllabus. Delaying inclusion of computers into the school curriculum until a certain grade level seems to be a maturational approach and not an emergent skills approach to computer education.

The children observed in the current study were offered access to computers at the age of 2 or 3. The parents decided by the child's interest and abilities when to initiate access to computers. These now 6-year-olds are comfortable with learning new skills and strategies for using computer hardware and software. The disparity of delaying access and opportunity to use computers in the home or school setting due to an arbitrary predetermined age seems counterproductive when attempting to prepare students to be capable technology savvy adults.

COMPUTERS IN SOCIETY

Young children grow in leaps and bounds physically, cognitively, socially, and emotionally. Parents and teachers serve the role of guardian as children travel on their voyage through childhood. The adults guiding children's acquisition of knowledge and learning experiences do not always agree on what tools and techniques should be part of the educational process. As computers have become ingrained into American culture there have been advocates promoting computer access for young children and proponents who warn of the damages that will be caused by exposing young children to computers. It is the responsibility of the adults living and working with children to evaluate and realize the advantages and detriments of using computers with young children.

According to Van Scoter, Ellis, and Railsback (2001) when computers are incorporated into young children's learning experiences in a developmentally appropriate manner there is an array of benefits which include:

- Computers are intrinsically motivating for young children, and contribute to cognitive and social development (NAEYC, 1996).
- Computers and software can serve as catalysts for social interaction and conversations related to children's work (Clements, Nastasi, & Swaminathan 1993).
- Computers can enhance children's self-concept and improve their attitudes about learning (Sivin-Kachala & Bialo, 1994).
- Children demonstrate increased levels of spoken communication and cooperation during computer use (Clements, 1994; Haugland & Wright, 1997).
- Children share leadership roles on the computer, and initiate interactions more frequently (Clements, 1994; Haugland & Wright, 1997).
- Computer play encourages longer, more complex speech and the development of fluency (Davidson & Wright, 1994).
- Young children interacting at computers engage in high levels of spoken communication and cooperation, such as turn-taking and peer collaboration.

- Compared to children in a similar classroom without computer experience, 3 and 4 year olds who used computers with supporting activities had significantly greater gains in verbal and nonverbal skills, problem solving, abstraction, and conceptual skills (Haugland, 1992).

Adults choosing appropriate software programs or child-oriented Internet web sites are using the computer to provide children with appropriate, positive learning experiences.

Haugland and Wright (1997) report the dangers that opponents of computer use with young children are concerned with, which are that computers:

- will replace other activity choices such as blocks or art
- will push children to learn new skills they are not ready to learn
- provide children with an unrealistic image of the real world
- are socially isolating
- reduce children's awareness of feelings and capacity for creativity

Research conducted by Attewell et al. (2003) validated critics' concerns that children who spent 8 or more hours a week using a home computer spent less time involved in sports or outdoor play, also resulting in young children with a heavier body mass index. The author is in favor of children being given access to computers. Further research is needed to gain a fuller portrayal of the benefits and dangers for young children's use of computers. It is important to understand the need for necessary time limits for computer use, the integration of computers into activity choices for children, and the possible physical impact on the growth and development of young children.

Parents in the current research study seemed to have found a balance between understanding the importance of their children gaining computer knowledge while incorporating computers as one of many options for their children's learning experiences. Parents and teachers select books, toys, puzzles, and other learning materials for children to play with. The computer is another tool and toy in the environment that adults offer children for entertainment or educational endeavors. It is not the tool itself, but rather how the computer is used with young children that will decide if the computer is *friend* or *foe*.

Gender Differences

By necessity women have used computers in the work setting since the 1970s. Many women are now choosing to use computers to shop on the Internet and for communicating by email with friends. Women are using computers as frequently as their male counterparts, but their recreational and entertainment choices do differ. Men and women spend comparable amounts of time using computers to complete college studies (Imhof, Vollmeyer, & Beierlein,

2007). The gender gap for women with computer use appears to have closed, as women are now using computers and venturing online (NCES, 2006).

Researchers such as Allen, Gur, and Benbow have "discovered structural and functional differences in male and female brains and gender-different approaches to learning and living that result primarily from brain differences, not environmental factors" (Gurian & Ballew, 2003, pp. 8–9). Although the sample size for the present study was small, there were several noteworthy observations regarding gender and computer use. Two of the boys in the study typically used the home computer with minimal assistance. These boys attended after-school computer classes once each week. Their parents did not remain in the area while they interacted with the computer. Assistance was offered when needed but overall, these boys worked independently as their skills were sufficient to do so. This difference in parental guidance may be due to chance, individual difference, or gender. Future research with a larger sample size could serve to clarify possible gender differences in computer knowledge and use.

Another gender-related topic that emerged during the study was the use of video games such as Game Boy. During interviews the parents of all three boys mentioned video games as a favorite recreational activity choice of their child. The parents of the three girls did not consider video games as an activity vying for the girls' attention. These parents do not seem to be familiar with possible educational benefits of mobile gaming that are available (Facer et al., 2003). Computers were discussed as having the potential to be educational while video games were considered a more frivolous form of entertainment. The possible educational benefits of incorporating video games into the school setting are being considered by educators and researchers (Sohn, 2004; Witt, 2007). The United States military is currently using video game simulations which focus on survival skills and teaching the Arabic language (Sullivan, 2004). As game play becomes part of the school curriculum, additional research is required to validate the capacity of video games as a useful educational tool.

There is an increase in children, both boys and girls, playing video games. Eighty-six percent of children today are gamers with global sales of video game consoles and software reaching $40 billion in 2004 (Center for Digital Education, 2007; Sullivan, 2004). Not only are computers and technology changing our world, but the change is occurring at an escalating rate. One aspect of the technological evolution is due to the convergence of services and technologies. For example, emails can be retrieved on a cellular telephone or on a computer. Cable television company providers are now offering telephone, Internet computer services, and voice over Internet Protocol (VoIP) telephones (Center for Digital Education, 2007). Services and technologies that were separated by devices or different companies are now intermingled. Research is required to investigate the convergence and possible usefulness of technology tools in educational settings.

Digital Divide and Digital Equity

In the mid-1990s as computers and the need for computer skills were becoming more prevalent in society, the problem of a *digital divide* was identified as the abyss between individuals with computer access and skills and those without (NCES, 2006). Factors that contribute to the disparity of access include demographics, socioeconomic status, race/ethnicity, family income, family members' educational levels, as well as issues of age and disability (NCES, 2006). Research conducted by Li, Atkins, and Stanton (2006) examined the effect of home and school computer use for Head Start children. The ability to use computers both at home and also at school had an additive effect on school readiness and cognitive development of children. Eliminating the digital divide could positively impact future educational attainment and career success for economically challenged children.

For some children an inequity exists in the ability to use, maintain, or fully engage with computers. At times, computers are present in the home or school setting; however, a knowledgeable adult may not be available to provide guidance and technology support. The nonprofit organization One Laptop Per Child (OLPC, 2008) is working toward placing crank laptop computers into the hands of children in third world countries. According to their web site, the organization views laptops as a wonderful way for all children to learn through independent interaction and exploration. This is an important step in creating a computer literate global society. The assistance of knowledgeable adults such as parents, teachers, or peers could allow children to further develop their computer knowledge, as guidance is an essential component of attaining computer literacy.

The issue of the digital divide is compounded by the looming quandary of providing digital equity for children using computers. The International Society for Technology in Education (ISTE) defines digital equity as "equal access and opportunity to digital tools, resources, and services to increase digital knowledge, awareness, and skills" (Davis et al., 2007, p. 8). Digital equity may not exist for some children who have access to computers in schools or public places but not at home. Lack of access to computers or lack of adults who are knowledgeable to assist with computer queries are possibilities for why inequities exist.

A conference was convened by ISTE (Davis et al., 2007) which examined critical issues pertaining to achieving digital equity for the 21st-century learner. The discussion focused on the challenges, solutions, and components that are essential for creating an environment that supports digital equity. According to ISTE, the stakeholders in the effort to achieve digital equity are teachers, community organizations, and businesses. The ISTE Digital Equity Summit (Davis et al., 2007, p. 10) resulted in participants offering a proposal with principles which would be required to move toward digital equity:

1. Legitimize the significant role culture plays in students' educational experiences.
2. Continue to challenge perceptions about the role of technology in education.
3. Encourage others to recognize the critical link between technology professional development and classroom practice.
4. Create opportunities for students to access technology outside of the classroom.
5. Continue to seek funding for technology in spite of challenges.

Providing children with laptops through the OLPC (2008) program and establishing principles to work toward achieving digital equity (Davis et al., 2007) are positive steps toward finding viable solutions to prepare children as literate citizens in a culture that is becoming increasingly dependent on computers (AAUW, 2000).

MEDIA TECHNOLOGY

Children and computers was the single technological focus for the current research. Other media technologies individually and collectively have been researched and new information is being unveiled about the advantages and detriments to American children. Media technology includes television, computers, cellular telephones, video games, iPods, instant messaging, virtual reality sites, and multiplayer video games. An in-depth report on research regarding children and electronic media was offered by The Future of Children, a collaboration of the Woodrow Wilson School of Public and International Affairs at Princeton University and the Brookings Institution (McLanahan, Haskins, Paxxon, Rouse, & Sawhill, 2008).

A key finding of the report is that the simultaneous use of different media, or media multitasking, by American youth is at an all-time high. Computers appear to be the central driver for this trend as the "media multitasking station" (McLanahan et al., 2008, p. 4). Parents and teachers are concerned as to how media technology will impact the cognitive development and academic achievement of children. According to the report, the constructive use of media technology offers educators a powerful teaching tool that will help children learn and have a positive impact on their behaviors.

The author agrees with The Future of Children findings for the subject of children and electronic media. It is not the type of technology or the amount of time children interact with media that need to be of concern to parents and teachers. It is *what* is being offered to children in the different platforms whether it is television, computer software, or video games. Adults are responsible for providing appropriate options for media choices and overseeing children's learning experiences. In the technological campaign to prepare young children to be computer literate, adults are a crucial variable to the equation.

Epilogue

This research of parents guiding their children at home computers is an inaugural step toward thinking about computer literacy from a developmental, emergent skills perspective. The view of emergent computer literacy through the Computer Literacy Development model proposed in this book is offered to spur discussion for the question: how does computer literacy develop in a young child? Employing an emergent skills approach for the subject of computer literacy frames the issue from a developmental perspective. The view that computer literacy develops in stages with emergent computer skills being first, early computer skills next and finally independent computer skills, is a constructivist perspective in which knowledge builds and grows. Socially mediated learning (Vygotsky, 1978), in this case a child being guided by an adult or more knowledgeable peer at the computer, is key to this developmental learning dynamic. Having a parent or teacher close by to scaffold learning at the computer is beneficial to a young child's emerging knowledge.

Opportunities for young children to independently engage with computers are also necessary for children to expand their computer expertise. Through experimentation and exploration the child *plays* with the computer, and the way computers work is revealed. When a child throws a basketball through a hoop over and over, the necessary angles, height, and force of throwing the ball in order to get a basket are eventually understood. It does not mean a child will always get the ball into the basket but the strategies needed to complete the task become evident through independent experimentation. The same chance for discovery is needed when a child is learning to use computers. A child needs time to explore software programs, wander around approved web sites, and operate the computer hardware on his or her own. A responsive adult who can offer assistance when computer challenges occur can ensure that a child will be able to remain engaged during computer activity time.

Parents participating in the current study had a positive influence on their children's sustained computer activity through varying levels of involvement. Parent problem solving skills, parent-child discourse, and parental awareness of children's computer activities were vital elements of each child's computer learning experience. The study results verify the importance of adult availability for guidance, encouragement, and monitoring of children's developing computer literacy.

Computers entered society as a new technology in the 1970s. As with other technologies such as radio and television, computers altered the existing social order, economy, and power structure of American society (Healy, 1998). Computers are now entrenched in our culture and the capability to use this cultural tool is essential for young children growing up in America today. In an April 2008 interview, Vivien Stewart, vice president for education at the New York City-based Asia Society, reflected on the challenges technology presents today that could not have been anticipated twenty five years ago. "Now, in the global and digital age, we need to rethink (again) what are the key things people need to know and be able to do" (Manzo & Cavanagh, 2008, p. 15). Knowing how to use a computer will have an impact on a child's educational experiences, social experiences, and future economic success. It is the responsibility of adults, both parents and educators, to guide young children's acquisition of computer literacy skills. In the Information Age, being computer literate is a proficiency that is critical in order to flourish in our technologically sophisticated world.

Appendices

APPENDIX A: COMPUTER ACTIVITY OBSERVATION SHEET

Date: Start Time:_____ End Time:_____

Child's Name:_____

Parent's Name_____

Computer Location:_____

Contextual Information: Initials:_____ ___

NOTES:

_____

_____

_____

_____

_____

_____

_____

_____

_____

_____

_____

_____

_____

_____

_____

_____

_____

_____

Initials:_____

APPENDIX B: PARENT COMPUTER PERSPECTIVE INTERVIEW

General Information

1. Tell me about your family. How many people are in your family? What is each person's gender, age, who works, who goes to school and where?
2. Tell me about the computer(s) in your household? Who uses a computer and for what?

Parent Computer Knowledge

3. Tell me about when and how you were first introduced to computers.
4. Tell me about how you were guided by someone else when you were learning to use computers.
5. Tell me about when and how you learned to use your home computer.
6. Tell me about where you have access to computers and what you mainly use computers for.
7. What do you do when you do not understand how to operate the hardware or software of a computer?

Child's Computer Knowledge

8. How was your child introduced to computers? Through school, at home, or at a friend's?
9. Tell me your memory of how your child began to understand how to use the computer. Who assisted and supported the child's learning and how?
10. What does your child do when he/she does not understand how to use the hardware or software of a computer?
11. Who guided your child's introduction to online computer use? How?
12. Where does your child have access to computers?

Cooperative Computer Use

13. When more than one person uses your home computer, do you find that using the computer together encourages cooperation or causes disagreements?
14. Tell me about when your child plays together with a friend on your home computer.

15. Tell me about when your child plays together with their friends on a computer at a friend's house.

Parental Perspective and Access to Computers

16. Do you think young children need to learn about how to use computers?
17. How do you think young children develop an understanding of how to use computers?
18. How do you think adults can provide children with access to computers?
19. What ways can adults guide children developing an understanding of how to use computers?
20. Is there anything else you would like to tell me about how you or your child developed an understanding of how to use computers, access to computers, or adults guiding young children at the computer?

APPENDIX C: VERBAL INSTRUCTIONS FOR PARENT INTERVIEW

As you know my name is Helen Mele Robinson and I am conducting research to explore how parents offer guidance and access to computers for young children. I have interview questions that I would like you to respond to. I am going to be asking you questions about computers, your child, and you. These questions are a guide but I may ask a related follow-up question to an answer that you may give. You can answer with as long of a response as needed to fully answer each question. Your participation is completely voluntary which means we can stop at any time if you decide you do not want to continue. Your responses will be confidential as I will not use actual names in any written information.

If any questions are not clear, please let me know so I may explain further what the question is asking. Your participation is appreciated and will hopefully add to the research in understanding how parents guide young children at the computer.

Thank you. We will now begin.

APPENDIX D: MELE ROBINSON CONTENT ANALYSIS CODING SHEET

Verbal/Nonverbal	Discourse Code	Adult Language Category	Comments

Discourse Codes
MI: Mother Inquiry
FI: Father Inquiry
CI: Child Inquiry
MD: Mother Discussion
FD: Father Discussion
CD: Child Discussion
MR: Mother Response
FR: Father Response
CR: Child Response
MF: Mother Feedback
FF: Father Feedback

Language Categories
CL: Conversational Language
IL: Inquiry Language
DL: Directive Language
VL: Validating Language
PL: Procedural Language

APPENDIX E: DEMOGRAPHICS

Child

Study child's age_____

Gender: Male_____ Female_____

Race _____

How many people live in household?_____

How may of these people are under the age 18? _____

Parents/Guardians

Male _____ Age ____ Race _____ Level of Education _____

Female ____ Age ____ Race _____ Level of Education _____

Highest level of education: Some high school/high school graduate/certificate program/2-year college/4-year college graduate/graduate degree

Marital Status _____(single, married, divorced, widowed, separated)

Family Income: Does child get school lunch services through Title I?

_____ Yes _____ No

APPENDIX F: NAEYC TECHNOLOGY POSITION STATEMENT

Technology and Young Children—Ages 3 through 8

In this position statement, we use the word technology to refer primarily to computer technology, but this can be extended to include related technologies, such as telecommunications and multimedia, which are becoming integrated with computer technology.

Technology plays a significant role in all aspects of American life today, and this role will only increase in the future. The potential benefits of technology for young children's learning and development are well documented (Wright & Shade, 1994). As technology becomes easier to use and early childhood software proliferates, young children's use of technology becomes more widespread. Therefore, early childhood educators have a responsibility to critically examine the impact of technology on children and be prepared to use technology to benefit children.

Market researchers tracking software trends have identified that the largest software growth recently has been in new titles and companies serving the early childhood educational market. Of the people who own home computers and have young children, 70% have purchased educational software for their children to use (SPA Consumer Market Report, 1996). While many new titles are good contributions to the field, an even larger number are not (Haugland & Shade, 1994).

Early childhood educators must take responsibility to influence events that are transforming the daily lives of children and families. This statement addresses several issues related to technology's use with young children: (1) the essential role of the teacher in evaluating appropriate uses of technology; (2) the potential benefits of appropriate use of technology in early childhood programs; (3) the integration of technology into the typical learning environment; (4) equitable access to technology, including children with special needs; (5) stereotyping and violence in software; (6) the role of teachers and parents as advocates; and (7) the implications of technology for professional development.

NAEYC's Position

Although now there is considerable research that points to the positive effects of technology on children's learning and development (Clements, 1994), the research indicates that, in practice, computers supplement and do not replace highly valued early childhood activities and materials, such as art, blocks, sand, water, books, exploration with writing materials, and dramatic play. Research indicates that computers can be used in developmentally appropriate ways beneficial to children and also can be misused, just as any tool can (Shade & Watson, 1990). Developmentally appropriate software offers opportunities for collaborative play, learning, and creation. Educators must use professional judgment in evaluating and using this learning tool appropriately, applying the same criteria they would to any other learning tool or experience. They must also weigh the costs of technology with the costs of other learning materials and program resources to arrive at an appropriate balance for their classrooms.

1.   In evaluating the appropriate use of technology, NAEYC applies principles of developmentally appropriate practice (Bredekamp, 1987) and appropriate curriculum and assessment (NAEYC & NAECS/SDE, 1992). In short, NAEYC believes that in any given situation, a professional judgment by the teacher is required to determine if a specific use of technology is age appropriate, individually appropriate, and culturally appropriate.

The teacher's role is critical in making certain that good decisions are made about which technology to use and in supporting children in their use of technology to ensure that potential benefits are achieved. Teachers must take time to evaluate and choose software in light of principles of development and learning and must carefully observe children using the software to identify both opportunities and problems and make appropriate adaptations. Choosing appropriate software is similar to choosing appropriate books for the classroom—teachers constantly make judgments about what is age appropriate, individually appropriate, and culturally appropriate. Teachers should look for ways to use computers to support the development and learning that occur in other parts of the classroom and the development and learning that happen with computers in complement with activities off the computer. Good teaching practices must always be the guiding goal when selecting and using new technologies.

2.   Used appropriately, technology can enhance children's cognitive and social abilities.

Computers are intrinsically compelling for young children. The sounds and graphics gain children's attention. Increasingly, young children observe adults and older children working on computers, and they want to do it, too. Children get interested because they can make things happen with computers. Developmentally appropriate software engages children in creative play, mastery learning, problem solving, and conversation. The children control the pacing and the action. They can repeat a process or activity as often as they like and experiment with variations. They can collaborate in making decisions and share their discoveries and creations (Haugland & Shade, 1990).

Well-designed early childhood software grows in dimension with the child, enabling her to find new challenges as she becomes more proficient. Appropriate visual and verbal prompts designed in the software expand play themes and opportunities while leaving the child in control. Vast collections of images, sounds, and information of all kinds are placed at the child's disposal. Software can be made age appropriate even for children as young as 3 or 4.

When used appropriately, technology can support and extend traditional materials in valuable ways. Research points to the positive effects of technology in children's learning and development, both cognitive and social (Clements, 1994; Haugland & Shade, 1994). In addition to actually developing children's abilities, technology provides an opportunity for assessment. Observing the child at the computer offers teachers a "window" onto a child's thinking. Just as parents continue to read to children who can read themselves, parents and teachers should both participate with children in computer activities and encourage children to use computers on their own and with peers.

Research demonstrates that when working with a computer children prefer working with one or two partners over working alone (Lipinski et al., 1986; Rhee & Chavnagri, 1991; Clements et al., 1993). They seek help from one another and seem to prefer help from peers over help from the teacher (King & Alloway, 1992; Nastasi & Clements, 1993). Children engage in high levels of spoken communication and cooperation at the computer. They initiate interactions more frequently and in different ways than when engaged with traditional activities, such as puzzles or blocks. They engage in more turn-taking at the computer and simultaneously show high levels of language and cooperative-play activity.

Technology extends benefits of collaboration beyond the immediate classroom environment for children in the primary grades who can already read and write. With the potential of access to the Internet or other online "user friendly" networks, young children can collaborate with children in other classrooms, cities, counties, states, and even countries. Through electronic field trips in real time or via diskette, children are able to share different cultural and environmental experiences. Electronic mail and telecommunications opportunities through the Internet facilitate direct communication and promote social interactions previously limited by the physical location of participating learners.

3. Appropriate technology is integrated into the regular learning environment and used as one of many options to support children's learning.

Every classroom has its own guiding philosophies, values, schedules, themes, and activities. As part of the teacher's overall classroom plan, computers should be used in ways that support these existing classroom educational directions rather than distort or replace them. Computers should be integrated into early childhood practice physically, functionally, and philosophically. Teachers can accommodate integration in at least five ways:

- Locate computers in the classroom, rather than in a separate computer lab (Davis & Shade, 1994).
- Integrate technology into the daily routine of classroom activity. For example, a teacher might introduce musical rhythm with actions, recordings, and a computer used as an electronic rhythm-matching game. The children then would work in small groups with the computer program serving as one of several learning centers.
- Choose software to enrich curriculum content, other classroom activities, or concepts. For example, the program in the computer learning center might allow children to invent their own rhythms that they could simultaneously hear played back and see displayed graphically. They could edit these rhythms on the computer, hearing and seeing the changes.
- Use technology to integrate curriculum across subject-matter areas. For example, one group of children used the computer to make signs for a restaurant in their dramatic-play area (Apple Computer Inc., 1993). The rhythm program helps children connect mathematical patterns to musical patterns.
- Extend the curriculum, with technology offering new avenues and perspectives. For example, exploring shapes on the computer provides opportunities to stretch, shrink, bend, and combine shapes into new forms. Such activities enrich and extend children's activities with physical manipulatives.

4.   Early childhood educators should promote equitable access to technology for all children and their families. Children with special needs should have increased access when this is helpful.

Educators using technology need to be especially sensitive to issues of equity.

A decade of research on the educational use of computers in schools reveals that computers maintain and exaggerate inequalities (Sutton, 1991). Sutton found gender, race, and social-class inequalities in the educational uses of computers, which Thouvenelle, Borunda, and McDowell summarize.

- Girls used computers in and out of school less often than did boys.
- African American students had less access to computers than did White students.
- Presence of computers in a school did not ensure access.
- Teachers, while concerned about equity, held attitudes that hindered access—they believed that better behaved students deserved more computer time and that the primary benefit of computers for low-achieving students was mastery of basic skills (i.e., drill-and-practice software).

- Richer schools bought more equipment and more expensive equipment (1994, p. 153–154).

These findings identify trends that, unchecked, will almost certainly lead to increased inequity in the future. Early childhood educators must find ways to incorporate technology into their classrooms that preserve equity of access and minimize or even reverse the current trends. For example, anecdotal reports indicate that preschool-age boys and girls show equal interest in computers, but as they grow older girls begin to spend less time with computers than do boys. There are a number of ways educators can proactively work to maintain girls' interest in computers and technology: (1) consider girls' interests and interaction styles when selecting and evaluating software for classroom use; (2) model the use of the computer as a learning and productivity tool and invite children, especially girls, to observe and assist them in the work; and (3) promote equity by offering special times for "girls only" use of computers, which permits girls to explore the computer without having to directly compete with boys (Thouvenelle et al., 1994).

Considerations of equity in curriculum content require qualitative judgments. For example, research evidence indicates that children who are economically disadvantaged have less access to computers at home and at-home access is related to attitudes and competence (Martinez & Mead, 1988). If schools wish to provide equity to children of low-income families, with respect to their confidence and competence concerning computer learning, these children need to be provided more in-school computer access (Sutton, 1991). And that access must be meaningful, moving beyond rote drill-and-practice usage.

Preschool-age children spend time in a variety of diverse settings (e.g., homes, child care centers, family child care), which further complicates the issues of equity and access. Some of these settings have considerable access to technology while others lack the very basics. The more early childhood educators believe in the benefits of appropriate use of technology at the preschool age, the more responsibility we bear in ensuring equity and access to this important learning tool.

Efforts should be made to ensure access to appropriate technology for children with special needs, for whom assistive technologies may be essential for successful inclusion.

For children with special needs, technology has many potential benefits. Technology can be a powerful compensatory tool—it can augment sensory input or reduce distractions; it can provide support for cognitive processing or enhance memory and recall; it can serve as a personal "on-demand" tutor and as an enabling device that supports independent functioning.

The variety of assistive-technology products ranges from low-tech toys with simple switches to expansive high-tech systems capable of managing complex environments. These technologies empower young children, increasing their independence and supporting their inclusion in classes with their peers. With adapted materials, young children with disabilities no longer have to be excluded from activities. Using appropriately designed and supported computer applications, the ability to learn, move, communicate, and recreate are within the reach of all learners.

Yet, with all these enhanced capabilities, this technology requires thoughtful integration into the early childhood curriculum, or it may fall far short of its promise. Educators must match the technology to each child's unique special needs, learning styles, and individual preferences.

5.   The power of technology to influence children's learning and development requires that attention be paid to eliminating stereotyping of any group and eliminating exposure to violence, especially as a problem-solving strategy.

Technology can be used to affirm children's diversity.

Early childhood educators must devote extra effort to ensure that the software in classrooms reflects and affirms children's diverse cultures, languages, and ethnic heritages. Like all educational materials, software should reflect the world children live in: It should come in multiple languages, reflect gender equity, contain people of color and of differing ages and abilities, and portray diverse families and experiences (Derman-Sparks & A.B.C. Task Force, 1989; Haugland & Shade, 1994).

Teachers should actively select software that promotes positive social values.

Just like movies and television today, children's software is often violent and much of it explicit and brutally graphic, as in most of the best-selling titles for the popular game machines. But, often, violence is presented in ways that are less obvious. In all of its forms, violence in software threatens young children's development and challenges early childhood educators, who must take active steps to keep it out of their classrooms (see the NAEYC Position Statement on Violence in the Lives of Children, 1994).

Some software programs offer children the opportunity to get rid of mistakes by "blowing up" their creations—complete with sound effects—instead of simply erasing or starting over. As a metaphor for solving problems or getting rid of mistakes, "blowing up" is problematic. In the context of a computer software experience, it is more troubling than in the context of television or video. Children control the computer software, and, instead of being passive viewers of what appears on the screen, with the computer they become active decision makers about what takes place on the screen. Software programs that empower children to freely blow up or destroy without thought of the actual consequences of their actions can further the disconnection between personal responsibility and violent outcomes.

Identifying and eliminating software containing violence is only one of the challenges facing early childhood educators. A related, opposite challenge is discovering software programs that promote positive social actions. For example, software has the potential to offer children opportunities to develop sensitivities to children from other cultures or to children with disabilities. Much could be done to help children develop positive responses to cultural and racial diversity by offering software programs that enable children to explore the richness within their own and different cultures.

6. Teachers, in collaboration with parents, should advocate for more appropriate technology applications for all children.

The appropriate and beneficial use of technology with young children is ultimately the responsibility of the early childhood educator, working in collaboration with parents. Parents and teachers together need to make better choices as consumers. As they become educated on the appropriate uses of technology, parents and teachers are more likely to make informed decisions and to make it known to developers of technology when they are unhappy with products. Working together, parents and teachers are a large consumer group wielding greater influence on the development of technology for young children. Following are specific recommendations for early childhood professionals as they advocate for more appropriate technology applications for all children.

- Provide information to parents on the benefits and use of appropriate software.
- Advocate for computer hardware that can be upgraded easily as new technology becomes available.
- Encourage software publishers to make previewing of software easier for parents and educators.
- Advocate for a system of software review by educators.
- Promote the development of software and technology applications that routinely incorporate features that cater to the needs of learners with different abilities.
- Advocate for software that promotes positive representation of gender, cultural and linguistic diversity, and abilities. Software publishers should create a balance of programs that appeal to both boys and girls.
- Encourage software publishers to create programs that support collaboration among learners rather than competition. Fostering cooperative learning enhances the acceptance of the abilities of all learners.
- Encourage software publishers to develop programs that reflect appropriate, nonviolent ways to solve problems and correct mistakes.

- Develop formal and informal information sharing and support for teachers, parents, and appropriate organizations and community-based programs. Encourage free community access to technology through libraries, schools, and so forth.
- Support policies on federal, state, and local levels that encourage funding that supports equity in access to technology for young children and their families.

7.   The appropriate use of technology has many implications for early childhood professional development.

As early childhood educators become active participants in a technological world, they need in-depth training and ongoing support to be adequately prepared to make decisions about technology and to support its effective use in learning environments for children.

To achieve the potential benefits of technology, both preservice and in-service training must provide early childhood educators with opportunities for basic information and awareness. These efforts must address the rapid proliferation and fast-paced change within the technology arena. Opportunities that emphasize evaluating the software in relation to children's development are essential.

Institutions of higher education and other organizations and groups that provide preservice and in-service education have a responsibility to

- incorporate experiences that permit educators to reflect on the principles of early childhood education and how technology can support and extend these principles;
- give teachers concentrated time to focus on how best to use educational technology and to develop a plan for the use of educational technology in a school or early childhood program;
- provide hands-on training with appropriate software programs to assist teachers in becoming familiar and comfortable with the operation and features of hardware and software; and
- provide on-site and school-based training on effectively integrating technology into the curriculum and assessment process.

At the classroom level, teachers need staff-development experiences (Kearsley & Lynch, 1992) that permit them to

- use teaching techniques that fully use the technology;
- encourage parental involvement with technology;
- match technology applications to the learning needs of individual children;
- look for cross-curriculum/cross-cultural applications;

- facilitate cooperative interactions among children; and
- use technology to improve personal efficiency.

The potentials of technology are far-reaching and ever changing. The risk is for adults to become complacent, assuming that their current knowledge or experience is adequate. "Technology is an area of the curriculum, as well as a tool for learning, in which teachers must demonstrate their own capacity for learning" (Bredekamp & Rosegrant, 1994, p. 61). As teachers try out their new knowledge in the classroom, there should be opportunities to share experiences and insights, problems and challenges with other educators. When teachers become comfortable and confident with the new technology, they can be offered additional challenges and stimulated to reach new levels of competence in using technology.

Early childhood educators should use technology as a tool for communication and collaboration among professionals as well as a tool for teaching children.

Technology can be a powerful tool for professional development. Software can provide accessible information and tools for classroom management, planning, and creation of materials. Telecommunications and the Internet can enable teachers to obtain information and new ideas from around the world and to interact with distant experts and peers. Early childhood educators can incorporate principles of cooperative learning as they assist distant peers in acquiring new skills; share curriculum ideas, resources, and promising practices; exchange advice; and collaborate on classroom and professional development projects. Providing training and support for access to services available via online networks and the Internet has the potential of opening the doors to worlds of additional classroom resources. With a responsive online system, mentors can assist novices in becoming more technology literate and more involved in actively using technology for professional benefits. As educators become competent users of technology for personal and professional growth, they can model appropriate use for young children.

Bibliography

Abdal-Haqq, I. (2001). *Constructivism in teacher education: Considerations for those who would link practice to theory*. Retrieved June 19, 2001, from http://www.ed.gov/databases/ERIC_Digests/ed426986.html

American Association of University Women Educational Foundation Commission on Technology, Gender, and Teacher Education. (2000). *Tech-savvy: Educating girls in the new computer age*. Washington, DC: American Association of University Women.

Apple Computer Inc. (1993). *The adventure begins: Preschool and technology* [Videocassette]. (Available from the National Association for the Education of Young Children)

Armstrong, A., & Casement, C. (2000). *The child and the machine: How computers put our children's education at risk*. Beltsville, MD: Robins Lane Press.

Attewell, P., Suazo-Garcia, B., & Battle, J. (2003, September). Computers and young children: Social benefit or social problem? *Social forces, 82*(1), 277–296.

Ba, H., Tally, B., & Tsikalas, K. (2002, February). *Children's emerging digital literacies: Investigating home computing in low-and middle-income families* (Center for Children and Technology Reports 1–51). Los Altos, CA: The David and Lucille Packard Foundation.

Bandura, A. (1986). *Social foundations of thought and actions: A social cognitive theory*. Englewood Cliffs, NJ: Prentice Hall.

Bandura, A., & Walters, R. (1963). *Social learning and personality development*. New York: Holt, Rinehart & Winston.

Bank Street College. (2008, April). *Literacy guide: Early literacy development*. Retrieved April 6, 2008, from http://www.bankstreet.edu/literacyguide/early.html

Becker, H. J. (1983). School uses of microcomputers: Report # 1 from a national survey. *Journal of computers in mathematics and science teaching, 3*(2), 29–33.

Becker, H. J. (1985). *How schools use microcomputers—Summary of the first national survey* (ERIC No. ED257448). Baltimore: The Johns Hopkins University Center for Social Organization of Schools.

Becker, H. J. (1994). *Analysis and trends of school use of information technologies*. Irvine, CA: Department of Education.

Becker, H. J. (2000, Fall/Winter). Who's wired and who's not: Children's access to and use of computer technology. In R. E. Behrman (Ed.), *The future of children: Children and computer technology, 10(20)* (pp. 44–75). Los Altos, CA: The David and Lucille Packard Foundation.

Behrman, R. E. (Ed.). (2002, Fall/Winter). Children and computer technology. In *The future of children, (10)2*. Los Altos, CA: The David and Lucille Packard Foundation.

Berk, L. E., & Winsler, A. (1995). *Scaffolding children's learning: Vygotsky and early childhood education.* Washington, DC: NAEYC.

Bitter, G. G., & Pierson, M. G. (2002). *Using technology in the classroom* (5th ed.). Boston: Allyn and Bacon.

Bogden, R. C., & Biklen, S. K. (1992). *Qualitative research in education* (2nd ed.).Boston: Allyn and Bacon.

Boitnott, K. (2007, July). Laptops and results. *Teacher magazine.* Retrieved April 6, 2007, from http://www.teachermagazine.org/tm/articles/2007/07/02/33tln_ boitnott_web.h18.html?tmp=2017280084

Bowman Alden, S. (2008). The role technology can play is preparing our children for the 21st century. *Computer learning foundation.* Retrieved April 22, 2008, from http://www.computerlearning.org/articles/Prepare.htm

Bredekamp, S., (Ed.). (1987). *Developmentally appropriate practice in early childhood programs serving children from birth through age 8* (Exp. ed.). Washington, DC: NAEYC.

Bredekamp, S., & Rosegrant, T. (1994). Learning and teaching with technology. In J. L. Wright & D. D. Shade (Eds.), *Young children: Active learners in a technological age* (pp. 53–61). Washington, DC: NAEYC.

Bronfenbrenner, U. (1989). Ecological systems theory. In R. Vasta (Ed.), *Annals of child development*: 6. Greenwich, CT: JAI, 187–251.

Bruner, J. S. (1990). *Acts of meaning.* Cambridge, MA: Harvard University Press.

Bruner, J. S. (1975). *Toward a theory of instruction.* Cambridge, MA: Harvard University Press.

Butzin, S. M. (2002, November/December). Project CHILD (Changing how instruction for learning is delivered): The perfect fit for multimedia elementary schools. *Multimedia schools, 9*(6), 14–16.

Cazden, C. (2001). *Classroom discourse: The language of teaching and learning* (2nd ed.). Portsmouth, NH: Heinemann.

Center for Digital Education. (2007). *Teaching the Millennials: A strategy paper from the Center for Digital Education.* Folsom, CA: e.Republic.

Chang, N., Rossini, M. L., & Pan, A.C. (1997). Perspectives on computer use for the education of young children. *Young Child: Technology and teacher education annual,* 1337–1340.

Chartock, R. (2000). *Educational Foundations: An Anthology.* Upper Saddle River, NJ: Prentice Hall.

Christie, J. F., Enz, B., & Vukelich, C. (2003). *Teaching language and literacy: Preschool through the elementary grades* (2nd ed.). Boston: Allyn and Bacon.

Clay, M. (1966). *Emergent reading behavior.* Unpublished doctoral dissertation, University of Auckland, New Zealand.

Clements, D. H. (1985). *Computers in early and primary education.* Upper Saddle River, NJ: Prentice Hall.

Clements, D. H. (1994). The uniqueness of the computer as a learning tool: Insights from research and practice. In J. L. Wright & D. D. Shade (Eds.), *Young children: Active learners in a technological age* (pp. 31–50). Washington, DC: NAEYC.

Clements, D. H. (1998, February). Young children and technology. In *Dialogue on early childhood science, mathematics, and technology education.* Washington, DC: Project 2061, American Association for the Advancement of Science.

Clements, D. H., Nastasi, B. K., & Swaminathan, S. (1993). Young children and computers: Crossroads and directions from research. *Young children, 48*(2), 56–64.

Coltman, P., Petyaeva, D., & Anghileri, J. (2002). Scaffolding learning through meaningful tasks and adult interaction. *Early years, 22*(1), 39–49.

Computer Literacy USA. (2007). *The computer literacy initiative.* Retrieved April 6, 2007, from http://www.virtualbill.net/clu/index.html

Cooper, J. D. (2000). *Literacy: Helping children construct meaning*. Boston: Houghton Mifflin.

Creswell, J. W. (2002). *Educational research: Planning, conducting, and evaluating quantitative and qualitative research*. Upper Saddle River, NJ: Merrill Prentice Hall.

Davidson, J. I. (1989). *Children & computers together in the early childhood classroom*. Albany, NY: Delmar Publishers Inc.

Davidson, J., & Wright, J. L. (1994). The potential of the microcomputer in the early childhood classroom. In J. L. Wright & D. D. Shade (Eds.), *Young children: Active learners in a technological age* (pp. 77–91). Washington, DC: NAEYC.

Davis, B. C., & Shade, D. D. (1994). *Integrate, don't isolate!—Computers in the early childhood curriculum*. (ERIC Digest December No. EDO-PS-94-17)

Davis, T., Fuller, M., Jackson, S., Pittman, J., & Sweet, J. (2007). *A national consideration of digital equity*. Washington, DC: International Society for Technology in Education. Retrieved January 4, 2008, from http://www.iste.org/digitalequity

Denzin, N. K. (1978). *The research act: A theoretical introduction to sociological methods* (2nd ed.). New York: McGraw-Hill.

Derman-Sparks, L., & The A.B.C. Task Force. (1989). *Anti-bias curriculum: Tools for empowering young children*. Washington, DC: NAEYC.

Deringer, D. K., & Molnar, A. R. (1982). Key components for a national computer literacy program. In R. J. Seidel, B. Hunter, & R. E. Anderson (Eds.), *Computer literacy: Issues and directions for 1985* (pp. 3–7). New York: Academic Press.

Dickinson, D. K., & Tabors, P. O. (Eds.). (2001). *Beginning literacy with language*. Baltimore: Paul H. Brookes Publishing Co.

Downes, T. I. (1998). Children's use of computers in their homes. *Dissertation abstracts international, 60*(03). (UMI No. 9922130)

Education Resource Information Center. (2008). Retrieved April 6, 2008, from http://www.eric.ed.gov/

Eggen, P., & Kauchak, D. (2001). *Educational psychology: Windows on classrooms* (5th ed.). Upper Saddle River, NJ: Prentice Hall.

Eisenberg, M. B., & Johnson, D. (1996). Computer skills for information problem-solving: Learning and teaching technology in context. *ERIC Digest*. Retrieved May 25, 2001, from http://ericr.syr.edu/ithome/digests/computerskills.html

Elkind, D. (1998, February). Educating young children in math, science, and technology. In *Forum on early childhood science, mathematics, and technology education* (pp. 1–14). Washington, DC: United States Department of Education.

Escobedo, T. H. (1992, May). Play in a new medium: Children's talk and graphics at computers. *Play and culture, 5.2*, 120–140.

Evans, J. (2007). *Tomorrow's students: Are we ready for the 21st-century learners?* EDUCAUSE 2007 Annual Conference. Retrieved April 1, 2008, from http://connect.educause.edu/blog/gbayne/e07podcasttomorrowsstuden/45344?time=1205005823

Facer, K., Furlong, J., Furlong, R., & Sutherland, R. (2003). *Screenplay: Children and computing in the home*. London: RoutledgeFalmer.

Fromberg, D. P. (2002). *Play and meaning in early childhood education*. Boston: Allyn and Bacon.

Gallagher, C. (2002). *Lev Semyonovich Vygotsky*. Retrieved July 5, 2002, from http://muskingum.edu/%7Epsychology/psycweb/history/vygotsky.htm

Gee, P. (2002). A sociocultural perspective on early literacy development. In S. B. Neuman & D. K. Dickinson (Eds.), *Handbook of early literacy research* (pp. 30–42). New York: Guilford Press.

Gurian, M. & Ballew, A. (2003). *The boys and girls learn differently: Action guide for teachers*. San Francisco: Jossey-Bass.

Hartcourt Education Company. (2007, April). Consider QWERTY . . . the typewriter keyboard. . . the universal user interface. *Connect newsletter.* Retrieved October 21, 2007, from http://home.earthlink.net/~dcrehr/whyqwert.html

Haugland, S. W. (1992). The effect of computer software on preschool children's developmental gains. *Journal of computing in childhood education, 3*(1), 15–30.

Haugland, S. W., & Shade, D. D. (1990). *Developmental evaluations of software for young children: 1990 edition.* New York: Delmar.

Haugland, S. W., & Shade, D. D. (1994). Software evaluation for young children. In J. L. Wright & D. D. Shade (Eds.), *Young children: Active learners in a technological age* (pp. 63–76). Washington, DC: NAEYC.

Haugland, S. W., & Wright, J. L. (1997). *Young children and technology.* Boston: Allyn and Bacon.

Healy, J. M. (1998). *Failure to connect: How computers affect our children's minds-and what we can do about it.* New York: Simon and Schuster.

Hobson, A. (Ed). (2007). Johann Heinrich Pestalozzi. In *The Columbia encyclopedia* (6th ed.). New York: Columbia University Press.

Imhof, M., Vollmeyer, R., & Beierlein, S. (2007). Computer use and the gender gap: The issue of access, use, motivation, and performance. *Computers in human behavior, 23*(6), 2823–2837.

Judge, S., Puckett, K., & Cabuk, B. (2004). Digital equity: New findings from the early childhood longitudinal study. *Journal of research on technology in education, 36*(4), 383–396.

Jukes, I. & Dosaj, A. (2003, February). The differences between digital native learners and digital immigrant teachers. Retrieved February 8, 2008 from http://www.cuyahoga.k12.oh.us/Flat_Pack/Digitial_Present/PDF.

Kaminski, J. A., Sloutsky, V. M., & Heckler, A. F. (2008). *Do children need concrete instantiations to learn an abstract concept?* Retrieved April 27, 2008, from http://cogdev.cog.ohio-state.edu/fpo644-Kaminski.pdf

Kearsley, G., & Lynch, W. (1992). Educational leadership in the age of technology: The new skills. *Journal of research on computing in education, 25*(1), 50–60.

Kennedy Manzo, K., & Cavanagh, S. (2008, April 23). America scouts overseas to boost education skills. *Education week, 1,* 14–16.

King, J. A., & Alloway, N. (1992). Preschooler's use of microcomputers and input devices. *Journal of educational computing research, 8,* 451–468.

King, K. P. (2002). *Keeping pace with technology.* Cresskill, NJ: Hampton Press Inc.

Kostelnik, M. J., Soderman, A. K., & Whiren, A. P. (1999). *Developmentally appropriate curriculum: Best practices in early childhood education.* Upper Saddle River, NJ: Merrill.

Land, M. L. (1999). Integrating the computer into the family: Influences on children'scomputer use in the home. *Dissertation abstracts international, 60*(05). (UMI No. 9928953)

Li, X., Atkins, M. S., & Stanton, B. (2006, April). Effects of home and school computer use on school readiness and cognitive development among head start children: A randomized controlled pilot trial. *Merrill-Palmer quarterly, 52*(2), 239–263.

Liang, P., & Johnson, J. (1999). Using technology to enhance early literacy through play. *Computers in the schools, 15*(1), 55–64.

Lipinski, J. A., Nida, R. E., Shade, D. D., & Watson, J. A. (1986). The effect of microcomputers on young children: An examination of free-play choices, sex differences, and social interactions. *Journal of educational computing research, 2*(2), 147–168.

Locke, L. L., Spirduso, W. W., & Silverman, S. J. (2000). *Proposals that work: A guide for planning dissertations and grant proposals* (4th ed.). ThousandOaks, CA: Sage Publications.

Lumpkins, B., Ryborn, K., Herrin, M., & Parker, F. (1995). Incorporating technology into a program for three- and four-year-old boys and girls. *Proceedings of the Society for Information Technology and Teacher Education Annual Conference, 265–267.*

Martens, P. (1996). *I already know how to read: A child's view of literacy.* Portsmouth, NH: Heinemann.

Martinez, M. E., & Mead, N. A. (1988). *Computer competence: The first national assessment.* (Tech report no. 17-CC-01). Princeton, NJ: National Educational Progress and Educational Testing Service.

Maxwell, J. A. (1996). *Qualitative research design: An interactive approach.* Thousand Oaks, CA: Sage Publications.

McCracken, G. (1988). *The long interview.* Newbury Park, CA: Sage Publications.

McLanahan, S., Haskins, R., Paxxon, C., Rouse, C., & Sawhill, I. (2008, Spring). Children and electronic media. *The future of children, 18*(1), 3–10.

McMillan, J. H. & Wergin, J. F. (2005). *Understanding and evaluating educational research.* (3rd ed.). Upper Saddle River, NJ: Prentice Hall.

Merriam, S. B. (1998). *Qualitative research and case study applications in education.* San Francisco: Jossey-Bass Publishers.

Morrow, L. M. (2001). *Literacy development in the early years: Helping children read and write.* Boston: Allyn and Bacon.

Moursund, D. (1982). Personal computing for elementary and secondary school students. In R. J. Seidel, R. E. Anderson, & B. Hunter (Eds.), *Computer literacy: Issues and directions for 1985* (pp. 73–84). New York: Academic Press.

Moursund, D. (2003). *A new definition of computer literacy.* Retrieved November 5, 2003, from http://darkwing.uoregon.edu/~moursund/dave/a_new_definition_of_comput.htm

Muffoletto, R., & Knupfer, N. N. (Eds.) (1993). *Computers in education: Social, political, and historical perspectives.* Cresskill, NJ: Hampton Press, Inc.

Nardi, P. M. (2003). *Doing survey research: A guide to quantitative methods.* Boston: Allyn and Bacon.

Nastasi, B.K., & Clements, D. H. (1993). Motivational and social outcomes of cooperative education environments. *Journal of computing in childhood education, 4*(1), 15–43.

National Association for the Education of Young Children. (1994). *Position statement on violence in the lives of children.* Washington, DC: Author.

National Association for the Education of Young Children. (1996). *Technology and young children—Ages 3 through 8.* Retrieved August 12, 2007, from http://www.naeyc.org/about/positions/PSTECH98.aspgov/nclb/overview/intro/execsumm.html

National Association for the Education of Young Children. (1997). *Developmentally appropriate practice in early childhood programs serving children from birth through age 8.* Retrieved August 12, 2007, from http://www.naeyc.org/about/positions/pdf/PSDAP98.PDF

National Association for the Education of Young Children, & National Association of Early Childhood Specialists in State Departments of Education. (1992). Guidelines for appropriate curriculum content and assessment in programs serving children ages 3 through 8. In S. Bredekamp & T. Rosegrant (Eds.), *Reaching potentials: Appropriate curriculum and assessment for young children, volume 1* (pp. 9–27). Washington, DC: NAEYC.

National Center for Education Statistics. (2001). Retrieved October 8, 2003, from http://nces.ed.gov/

National Center for Education Statistics. (2006, September). *Computer and Internet use by students in 2003: Statistical analysis report.* Retrieved October 21, 2007, from http://nces.ed.gov/pubs2006/2006065.pdf.

National Commission on Excellence in Education (1983). *A nation at risk: The imperative for educational reform.* Washington, DC: United States Department of Education.

National Institute of Child Health and Human Development. (2000). Report of the National Reading Panel. Teaching children to read: An evidence-based assessment of the scientific research literature on reading and its implications for reading instruction (NIH Publication No. 00–4769). Washington, DC: U.S. Government Printing Office.

No Child Left Behind Act of 2001. (2002) (P.L. 107–110). Retrieved October 19, 2005, from http://www.ed.gov/nclb/landing.jhtml?src=ln

North Central Regional Educational Laboratory. (2002). Vygotsky, Piaget and Bruner. Retrieved July 5, 2002 from http://www.ncrel.org/sdrs/areas/issues/methods/instrctn/in51k2-4.htm.

Northwest Territories Literacy Council. (2008, April). *Supporting literacy development at different ages and stages.* Retrieved April 6, 2008 from http://www.nald.ca/library/learning/nwt/develop/develop.pdf

Nye, J. S., Jr., & Owens, W. A. (1996). America's information edge. *Foreign affairs, 75*(2), 20–36.

One Laptop Per Child. (2008). Retrieved April 18, 2008, from http://www.laptop.org/vision/index.shtml

Pajares, F. (2004). *Albert Bandura: Biographical sketch.* Retrieved April 6, 2008, from http://des.emory.edu/mfp/bandurabio.html

Papert, S. (1980). *Mindstorms: Children, computers, and powerful ideas.* New York: Basic Books.

Papert, S. (1993). *Mindstorms: Children, computers, and powerful ideas* (2nd ed.). New York: Basic Books.

Patton, M. Q. (2002). *Qualitative research & evaluation methods* (3rd ed.). Thousand Oaks, CA: Sage Publications.

Pollard, A., & Tann, S. (1993). *Reflective teaching in the primary school* (2nd ed.). London: Continuum International Publishing Group.

Prensky, M. (2001a). Digital native, digital immigrants. *On the horizon (9)5, 1–6.*

Prensky, M. (2001b). Digital native, digital immigrants, Part II: Do they really think differently? *On the horizon (9)5, 1–9.*

Puckett, M. B., & Black, J. K. (2001). *The young child: Development from prebirth through age eight* (3rd ed.). Upper Saddle River, NJ: Prentice Hall.

Raingruber, B. (2003). Video-cued narrative reflection: A research approach for articulating tacit, relational, and embodied understandings. *Qualitative health research, 13,* 1155–1169.

Rhee, M. C., & Chavnagri, N. (1991). *4-year-old children's peer interactions when playing with a computer.* (ERIC Document Reproduction Service No. ED342466.

Roblyer, M. D. (2003). *Integrating educational technology into teaching.* UpperSaddle River, NJ: Pearson Education.

Rogers, E. M., McManus, J. H., Peters, J. D., & Kim, J. I. (1985). The diffusion of microcomputers in California high schools. In M. Chen. & W. Paisley (Eds.), *Children and microcomputers: Research on the newest medium* (pp.151–169). Beverly Hills, CA: Sage Publications.

Rosberg, M. (1995, May). Young children and literacy. *Proceedings of the Study Conference on Cued Speech in Malay, Malaysia,* 2–12.

Shade, D. D., & Watson, J. A. (1990). Computers in early education: Issues put to rest, theoretical links to sound practice, and the potential contribution of micro-worlds. *Journal of educational computing research, 6*(4), 375–392.

Shields, M. K., & Behrman, R. E. (2000, Fall/Winter). Children and computer technology: Analysis and recommendations. In R. E. Behrman (Ed.), *The future of children: Children and computer technology, 10(2)* (pp. 4–30). Los Altos, CA: The David and Lucille Packard Foundation.

Shonkoff, J. P., & Phillips, D. A. (2000). *From neurons to neighborhoods: The science of early childhood development.* Washington, DC: National Academy Press.

Silvern, S. B. (1998). Educational implications of play with computers. In D. Fromberg & D. Bergen (Eds.), *Play from birth to twelve and beyond: Contexts, perspectives, and meanings* (pp. 530–536). New York: Garland.

Siraj-Blatchford, J., & Whitebread, D. (2000). Supporting information and communication technology in the early years. In *Supporting early learning series* (pp. 1–14). Berkshire, UK: Open University Press.

Sivin-Kachala, J., & Bialo, E. R. (1994). *Report on the effectiveness of technology in schools, 1990–1994.* Washington, DC: Software Publishers Association. (ERIC Document Reproduction Service No. ED371726)

Slegers, B. (1996, March). A review of the research and literature on emergent literacy. *Viewpoints.* Retrieved April 6, 2008, from http://www.eric.ed.gov/ERICDocs/data/ericdocs2sql/content_storage_01/0000019b/80/14/a2/8b.pdf

Soderman, A. K., Gregory, K. M., & O'Neill, L. T. (1999). *Scaffolding emergent literacy: A child-centered approach for preschool through grade 5.* Boston: Allyn and Bacon.

Software Publishers Association. (1996). Consumer market report. Washington, DC: Author.

Sohn, E. (2004, January). What video games can teach us. *Science news for kids.* Retrieved October 8, 2007, from http://www.sciencenewsforkids.org/articles/20040121/Feature1.asp

Staten Island Census Statistics. (2005). *United States Census Bureau.* Retrieved August 31, 2005, from http://factfinder.census.gov/servlet/SAFFFacts?_event=Search&geo_id=&_geoContext=&_street=&_county=1012&_cityTown=1012&_state=&_zip=&_lang=en&_sse=on&pctxt=fph&pgsl=010

Steward, E. P. (1995). *Beginning writers in the zone of proximal development.* Hillsdale, NJ: Lawrence Erlbaum Associates.

Storch, S. A., & Whitehurst, G. J. (2001). The role of family and home in the literacy development of children from low-income backgrounds. *New directions for child and adolescent development, 92,* 53–71.

Sullivan, A. (2004, November). *Video games teach more than hand-eye coordination.* Retrieved April 21, 2008, from http://education.mit.edu/papers/seriousgames.htm

Sulzby, E., & Teale, W. (1996). Emergent literacy. In R. Barr, M. Kamill, P. Mosenthal, & P. D. Pearson (Eds.), *Handbook of reading research: Vol. 2* (pp. 727–758). New York: Longman.

Sutton, R. E. (1991). Equity and computers in the schools: A decade of research. *Review of educational research, 61*(4), 474–505.

Taylor, D. (1983). *Family literacy: Young children learning to read and write.* Portsmouth, NH: Heinemann.

Taylor, D., & Dorsey-Gaines, C. (1988). *Growing up literate: Learning from inner-city families.* Portsmouth, NH: Heinemann.

Teale, W. H. (1986). Home background and young children's literacy development. In W. H. Teale & E. Sulzby (Eds.), *Emergent literacy: Writing and reading* (pp. 173–206). Norwood, NJ: Ablex.

TechTerms.com. (2008). *The online computer dictionary.* Retrieved June 12, 2007, from http://www.techterms.com/definition/computer

Thouvenelle, S., Borunda, M., & McDowell, C. (1994). Replicating inequities: Are we doing it again? In J. L. Wright & D. D. Shade (Eds.), *Young children: Active learners in a technological age* (pp. 151–166). Washington, DC: NAEYC.

Tuckman, B. W. (1999). *Conducting educational research* (3rd ed.). Fort Worth, TX: Harcourt Brace College Publishers.

United States Census Bureau. (2003). *Current Population Survey Report. Computer and internet use in the United States: 2003.* Retrieved June 12, 2007, from http://www.census.gov/population/www/socdemo/computer.html

United States Department of Education. (1996). *Technology literacy challenge.* Retrieved May 25, 2001, from http://ed.gov/Technology/Plan/NatTechPlan/priority.html

United States Department of Education. (2002). *Enhancing education through technology.* Retrieved August 15, 2002, from http://ed.gov/inits/nclb/partx.html

United States Department of Education. (2005). *National Education Technology Plan.* Retrieved May 6, 2005, from http://www.nationaledtechplan.org/theplan/ANationontheMove.asp

Urban Dictionary. (2008). *Generation z.* Retrieved April 12, 2008, from http://www.urbandictionary.com/define.php?term=generation+z

Van Hoorn, J., Monighan Nourot, P., Scales, B., & Rodriquez Alward, K. (2003). *Play at the center of curriculum.* Upper Saddle River, NJ: Prentice Hall.

Van Scoter, J., Ellis, D., & Railsback, J. (2001, June). *Technology in early childhood education.* Northwest Regional Educational Laboratory, Portland, OR: Office of Educational Research and Improvement. Retrieved April 21, 2008, from http://www.netc.org/earlyconnections/byrequest.html

VanSlyke, T. (2003, May/June). Digital natives, digital immigrants: Some thoughts from the generation gap. *The technology source.* Retrieved April 25, 2008, from http://ts.mivu.org/default.asp?show=article&id=1034

Vygotsky, L. S. (1962). *Mind in society.* Cambridge, MA: Harvard University Press.

Vygotsky, L. S. (1978). *Thought and language.* Cambridge, MA: MIT Press.

Wartella, E. A., & Jennings, N. (2000, Fall/Winter). Children and computers: New technology—old concerns. In R. E. Behrman (Ed.), *The future of children: Children and computer technology, 10(20)* (pp. 31–43). Los Altos, CA: The David and Lucille Packard Foundation.

Wartella, E. A., & Reeves, B. (1983). Recurring issues in research on children and media. *Educational Technology, 23,* 5–9.

Wasik, B. H., Dobbins, D. R., & Herrmann, S. (2002). Intergenerational family literacy: Concepts, research, and practice. In S. B. Neuman & D. K. Dickinson (Eds.), *Handbook of early literacy research* (pp. 444–459). New York: Guilford Press.

Watt, D. H. Education for citizenship in a computer-based society. In *Computer literacy: Issues and directions for 1985,* R. J. Seidel, R. E. Anderson, and B. Hunter, Eds. Academic Press, New York, 1982. pp. 53–68.

Webster, A., & Feiler, A. (1998). The patterning of early literacy events in ten family contexts and their visibility to teachers. Research papers in education: Policy and practice, *13*(3), 231–260.

Whitehead, A. N. (1957). *Aims of education.* New York: The Free Press.

Whitehurst, G. J., & Lonigan, C. J. (1998). Child development and emergent literacy. *Child Development, 69,* 848–872.

Wiegel, D. J., Martin, S. S., & Bennett, K. K. (2006). Contributions of the home literacy environment to preschool-aged children's emerging literacy and language skills. *Early childhood development and care,* 176(3&4), 357–378.

Witt, H. (2007, February 11). Skip the textbook, play the video game. *Chicago Tribune.* Retrieved April 6, 2008, from http://www.cyberfest.us/Education/Skip%20the%20textbook%20play%20the%20videogame%20Chgo%20Trib%202-11-07.pdf.

Wright, J. L., & Shade, D. D. (Eds.). (1994). *Young children: Active learners in a technological age.* Washington, DC: NAEYC.

Index